Accepting Trust

The Critical Role of Independent School Trustees

*To Marri
With appreciation
for all you do*

To

My friend, editor and wife, Pat, who lived with me through the events that engendered this book, and who has her own organizational stories to tell.

Accepting Trust

The Critical Role of Independent School Trustees

Donald D. Mordecai

Polyglot Press

Philadelphia

THIS IS A POLYGLOT PRESS EDUCATION EDITION
Published in the United States by Polyglot Press, Inc.

A member of Polyglot Press Alliance

Philadelphia • Barcelona • Beijing • Rio de Janeiro • Toronto • London •

Sydney • Cairo • Tel Aviv • Mexico DF • Moscow • Trivandrum

Copyright ©2009 by Donald D. Mordecai

All rights reserved under International and Pan-American Copyright Conventions.

No parts of this book may be reproduced or utilized in any means, electronic, mechanical, including photocopying, recording, information storage-retrieval, or other without permission of the copyright holder.

Accepting Trust: The Critical Role of Independent School Trustees

By Donald D. Mordecai. Trade Paper

ISBN 10: 1-4115-9976-4
ISBN 13: 978-1-4115-9976-5

Polyglot Press, the portrayal of the parrot on a perch, and the portrayal of a magnifying glass with the words "high legibility typeface" in the lens, and the portrayal of a computer monitor with the words "custom typeset" on the screen are all trademarks of Polyglot Press, Inc.

This book is printed on acid-free paper. Designed for readability using Adobe Minion type family.

Library of Congress
Cataloging-in-Publication Data
Library of Congress Cataloging-in-Publication Data

Mordecai, Donald D., 1938-
  Accepting trust : the critical role of independent school trustees / Donald D. Mordecai.
    p. cm.
  ISBN-13: 978-1-4115-9976-5 (trade paper : alk. paper)
  ISBN-10: 1-4115-9976-4 (trade paper : alk. paper)
  1. School boards. 2. School management and organization. I. Title.
  LB2831.M67 2009
  379.1'531--dc22
                              2009027537

Composition by Polyglot Press, Inc., Philadelphia, PA. www.polyglotpress.com

Printed in the United States of America

Table of Contents

Dedication		iii
Acknowledgements		ix
Preface		xi
Introduction		xv
1.	School Organization: The Board of Trustees	1
2.	School Organization: The Administration	15
3.	The Head of School and the Board	21
4.	The Role of the Chief Financial Officer	29
5.	The Business of Education	35
6.	Endowment Management	47
7.	Planning	53
8.	Mission Statements	59
9.	Assessment and Mission Review	67
10.	Negotiating Change	73
11.	Technology – A Speculation for Thoughtful Trustees	81
Appendix A: Essential School Elements: a loose Glossary		85

Acknowledgements

The people who work in schools are generally committed, thoughtful and caring. I have been fortunate in my colleagues over the years and have learned from each of them.

They are, of course, not responsible for the observations and conclusions in this book and probably would not agree with at least some of them. Nevertheless I want to acknowledge some out of a much larger possible list from whom I learned a lot about organizational dynamics in general and the operation of school boards in particular.

Trustees David Cohen, Lynn Edens, Bob Fleishman, Fred Lione and Jack Heilshorn helped me to understand what boards needed to know to make informed decisions.

I learned the importance in nonprofits of teamwork from administrators Lea Dmytryck, Diane Spence and Tom Tinker.

From Jim Saltonstall and Rick Belding I got good advice as I was starting this journey and from Mark Brossman great support during some difficult school days.

Marjo Talbott taught me a great deal about transforming schools and I am grateful as well for her collegiality and trust.

Preface:

When I retired from my last school I contemplated a new season of life without board meetings. I had, shall we say, an unrealistic view of a life building furniture, growing vegetables, spending time on the water, playing tennis and all the rest of that familiar dream. Six months after I left the school, I found myself consulting to the board of a new school: literally a startup. The concept was great; the timing turned out to be awful, as the credit market dried up, donors headed for the hills and the economy tanked.

Nevertheless, the board of this startup kept on and demonstrated again the behavior described in these essays: passion trumps rational behavior. The board hired an administrator with no experience running a school, spent money on real estate firms to find a facility for the new school that they could not afford and, eventually, ran out of donors and money. Then, after board members had spent nearly three years and I had worked with them for over a year and a half to make this all work, I helped them to shut it down.

The board leadership, however, did not quit. But now, without a head or staff and with critical members unwilling to continue to support the project the leadership forged quixotically on. They were still convinced they could raise significant money and make real estate deals that would result in the realization of their dream. Meanwhile, as of this writing, the economy is getting worse, not better, and the likelihood of significant new money for a startup, no matter the validity of the concept, seems dim.

This is not to criticize chasing a dream. There is a conundrum here: unless there is passion, the big dreams are never dreamed and never realized. Yet, in today's reality, unless the dream is subject to a clear-eyed analysis it will fail. It is probably no longer possible to found a school with a handful of students and a teacher in a drawing room or church basement, as so many schools were founded. So it is not that the dream is unrealistic; it is that the dream, without that analysis, is simply a dream. It will not be there when the board wakes up.

While working with the board and then with the head, I watched their actions and interactions and now, with hindsight, can see how the truth of the essays in this book plays out. Because I was a consultant, working far from the place the school was planned for, I had a certain detachment that I could not have had when I wrote the various essays on boards and schools. It was clear that decisions were driven by personalities rather than analysis. Egos trumped strategy. Even the hard-core realists felt a commitment to the idea of the new school and, while criticizing the decision process (such as it was), could not themselves give up the dream.

There is a balancing act required in successful, innovative institutions: there must be a dream, but there must be a willingness to test the elements of the dream against an objective reality. Both elements are required. Obviously, it is easier to say than to do. Dreams are fragile and require the right conditions of support. Some reality must be suspended. But once dreamt, the dream must be carefully cosseted, and at the same time be subjected to careful analysis.

Where boards go wrong, I believe, is in the failure to provide for both dreams and analysis without criticism. Dreamers cannot be told (or made to feel) that their dreams are childish, unrealistic and irrelevant. The realists cannot be told (or made to feel) that their analysis is negative or that it fails to support the dream and the team. Boards often marginalize the realists and the realists are often unable to confront the dreamers because, paradoxically, the realists also support the dream.

The premise of this book is that boards require entire persons. They cannot succeed as only dreamers or only realists. Their failures are a result of leaving some of their passions and intellect at the boardroom door. It is hard to carry the weight of the trust of the responsibility, but that is the job of a trustee and it takes the engagement of the whole person, both passionate and realistic. That is the premise I want to support.

The consulting job did not change my thoughts about schools and trustees. It did further validate the need for trustees to resist being only cheerleaders or critics and to approach their responsibility open to other viewpoints and interests with an enlightened view of reality.

If trustees were to accept that role, there would be many fewer contests between boards and heads and many more successful and effective schools.

Introduction:
The Need for Activist Trustees

Election to the board of a nonprofit school is a serious matter. It carries legal and moral responsibilities for the long-term viability of the organization. Trustees have the authority as well as the duty to ensure that the trust for which they are responsible not only survives but stays true to its mission.

Far too often trustees accept their role without understanding the requirements of the stewardship. This series of essays is designed to help trustees understand the dimensions of that trust and to suggest some ways to carry out their responsibilities as trustees.

Trustees guide the future of their schools in a competitive environment that can and has put institutions out of business. That competition is not only other similar schools; it is a growing range of "education providers." As schools become more and more expensive, alternatives become increasingly attractive. The potential of the Internet and World Wide Web to deliver content is stunning. If these high priced schools are to survive, they will have to get much better than many of them are, which means better and broader content and better delivery of that content. Addressing those issues is the primary responsibility of the board of trustees and its chief executive officer, the head of school. It is hard work that many boards and heads are not prepared to do.

This volume addresses the administration and governance of independent schools, by which I mean specifically members of the National Association of Independent Schools (among whose members I worked for many years). The audience is, of course, larger than that subset of private schools. Criticism that follows is not of the value and importance of the missions these organizations undertake, nor of individual trustees and administrators. They generally do their best to support the institution—as they understand their roles—but wasted energy and resources reduce or undercut their ability to deliver services. It is precisely because their missions are so important that sloppy articulation of mission and poor management of resources is so distressing. The primary object of the criticism is the boards of trustees because they have the legal and moral responsibility for their institutions.

I worked at a seminary as an interim business manager for a year and a half, at a boarding school for special needs adolescents, and at two urban nursery through 12th grade schools over a sixteen-year period in various administrative roles. I learned an enormous amount at each school and valued the commitment of many teachers, administrators, parents and board members. At the same time I was aware of how much better each institution could have been if it were well and carefully focused on sustainable goals and objectives which were understood and supported by its constituencies.

The following illustrations and comments are based on my experience with my schools, on conversations with other administrators, teachers and parents, and on my reading of a number of books and articles on nonprofits. The illustrations have been generalized; they do not purport to describe history at any specific institution. Similarly, my comments and suggestions are not meant to be criticisms of specific schools or individuals, but rather illustrative of general situations. I hope they are helpful.

I believe that management of independent schools should be validated by measurement of outcomes. In businesses, outcomes are measured in units produced or sold and ultimately in earnings. A school exists, as is true of all nonprofits, "to bring about a change in individuals and in society."[1] The agents of change are not machines but people. The critical question is how to measure the outcomes against benchmarks that the agents of change will accept. This is a problem for schools because of the number of entities to which the organization is accountable and because of the perceived difficulty of defining and measuring outcomes. Because of these perceived difficulties, there is in practice no acceptable way for teachers to get objective feedback on their success. Since it is hard to feel successful in an environment where the criteria for success are elusive, schools and their employees are fragile. This fragility results in a structure that is resistant to change and paradoxically is hostile to measurement, the very thing that could help its members feel successful.

It could be different. Measurement of the success of the nonprofit organization is possible in financial terms, just as it is for profit-making companies. Measurement of outcomes in organizations is always indirect. The success of a fishing rod maker is not measured by how well the rod casts but by net income and return on investment. While profit is not a usual measure of a nonprofit school, a continuing negative net income will eventually force it to close. Businesses ultimately measure net profit and return on investment (ROI) and stock price, but they also use intermediate measures of success: inventory turnover, cost of goods produced, employee turnover, volume and many other measures. Schools can also set and measure intermediate benchmarks by which to measure their success. The board needs benchmarks to assess how well it is carrying out its responsibility. That is the specific subject of the chapter on Assessment and Mission Review.

Independent schools are very expensive, especially those not subsidized by churches or by the time and in-kind contributions of the parents. The reasons for the cost of private education are often not explicit and may have very little to do with the quality of education provided. Some of the reasons for that cost may be poor information, weak management and inadequate accountability.

A few examples may help to illustrate the motivation for these essays. They may help to provide some background for later conclusions and suggestions.

- *On a June morning, two weeks before the close of its fiscal year when essentially all of the revenue had been collected and virtually all of the bills for the year paid, the finance committee of the board was trying to discover from the business manager whether there would be a surplus of approximately $500,000 or a deficit of roughly the same amount. The business manager did not know. There was, as it turned out, a surplus.*

• In August, a groundbreaking took place for the renovation of a building for which the only cost estimate was the bid price from a single contractor. The "budget" did not include architect's fees, the removal of known asbestos, or the cost of bringing water from the street for the required sprinkler system. The final cost of the renovation was, of course, well over budget.

• In late November the head of school was still hiring staff for the current year, because it was noticed that sections at certain grade levels were too large and needed to be divided. When the same practice continued in the fall of the next year, with no predictable staffing plan, it was suggested that realistic budget making was impossible until the school could, with some accuracy, predict its enrollment and establish a staffing plan to support that enrollment.

Although dismissed as an impossible task, a fairly cursory analysis showed that enrollment at grades 10 through 12 followed an extremely stable pattern, based directly on 9th grade enrollment. With predictable enrollment by grade, it was then possible to develop an efficient staffing plan.

There are well-managed excellent schools with happy kids and strong faculties and a good college admissions record. Some of them approach education with respect for the individual student and teacher. Some can articulate their organizational and educational goals, and some have figured out how to measure their success relative to those goals. Some are in that happy state because of careful analysis and planning by an involved and committed board, implemented by a strong administration supported and carefully evaluated by that board. Most schools try to build on their perceived strengths and to correct weaknesses, but usually struggle to do so.

Successful schools have clear and measurable missions, developed with the leadership of the board. The board, acting in partnership with the school's head, administration and faculty, also ensures that the institution understands its mission. Successful schools are not afraid to measure organizational outcomes against their mission nor to make changes to the processes or to the mission as experience and analysis dictates. The board holds the core values of the community dear, but understands that over the long haul, those values may be expressed within a variety of structures with a variety of outcomes.

[1] Druker, Peter. *Managing the Non-Profit Organization.* New York: Harper Business, 1992, p. 3.

Chapter 1

School Organization: The Board of Trustees

Schools organized as 501(c)(3) nonprofit corporations are "owned" by a self-perpetuating board of trustees which is legally responsible for the governance of the school and for safeguarding its permanent assets (endowment and facilities).

The board sets policies and hires a head of school to carry out those policies. The board has an obligation to evaluate how well assets are used to support the school's goals, to ensure that its policies are being properly implemented and to make sure that the school complies with all appropriate codes, laws and regulations. Board members have a duty to make reasonable inquiries to assure themselves that they are carrying out their fiduciary responsibilities. In order to carry out their individual and collective duties, they must understand and exercise their responsibility for oversight of the operation and responsibility for the long-term viability of the school.

Minding the Future

It is critical to educate board members to understand that their trust is almost entirely future-driven. Successful boards understand that responding solely to current demands is not responsible governance. Boards tend to be involved in current concerns because their involvement with the organization is focused on the current, as parents, past parent or graduates. But tomorrow quickly becomes today; and without adequate understanding of tomorrow, the institution will not be ready – competitive – when the future has arrived. It is not easy to train and energize a board to think constructively about the future, but that is what they must do: It is the only way that the board can do the evaluation and planning required to carry out its trust.

When selecting people to serve on the board, their ability to consider the needs of the future and to think through what those needs will mean to the institution over time is an asset. That sort of leadership will help minimize risk and assuage those who are naturally threatened by change (faculty, graduates, families relatively new to the school). At the same time these men and women must keep their eyes and brains finely attuned to what is currently exciting and satisfying so that change will generate similar excitement and satisfaction 10 and 20 years into the future when the demands, needs and competition will all have changed again.

Because the board designs the school's future, it would be helpful to have trustees who are brought in specifically because of their experience with the bigger picture, and have some experience also with transforming organizations. They can be educators, CEOs, lawyers, just like many of the members of the existing board, which is often comprised of parents, graduates and other insiders, but will have a more objective view of the school and will understand that their specific role is to help the board think about and plan for the future.

Since schools do not pay their board members, these outside members will have to have some interest in and connection with the school, or with the head or board president that will interest them in the job and keep them willing to stay with it. It should be understood, of course, that the process of working with a school determined to think through its mission and how it can set goals and measure its progress toward those goals will be an interesting place to be. It is important work and can be very satisfying to all of those who participate, whether they are insiders or outsiders.

As boards struggle to define their roles, members are often frustrated in the process.

> Most people who come onto the board of a ... (nonprofit) organization bring substantial life experiences plus skills from other roles in their lives, such as business or professional practice. They accept the position with the hope ... that their skills will be used to serve a cause about which they care deeply.

> Soon, however, they confront the realities of endless meetings and wandering discussions of ambiguously identified issues only

tangentially related to the important matters of the organization. Grousing in the hallway or parking lot after the meeting is about as far as they go with their discontents. Some people accept the limitations implicit in the group's behavior, while others leave the role disillusioned and disappointed.... Few see clear avenues or tools with which they might work to make substantial changes in the quality of the work of the board.

Although boards are responsible for the well being of their organizations, their specific local duties are often ambiguous and usually there are few penalties for poor performance.... Few members can articulate clear expectations or criteria for board performance, and few boards ever take the time to evaluate their own efforts and draw conclusions about how well they are adding value to their organizations. As a result, many boards of ... organizations under perform and many of their members are dissatisfied with the quality or impacts of their efforts.[1]

Or, as stated at the end of *Governance as Leadership*: "We believe that nonprofit boards face a problem of purpose, not a problem of performance."[2]

Members of the board of trustees of a nonprofit organization join its board primarily to support the cause of that organization and because they resonate to the ethos of the organization. Trustees, like the rest of us, operate in their own self-interest; when the values of the institution are congruent with the values of the trustee, he or she will feel comfortable and, in a sense, supported by the organization, just as the institution is supported by the trustee.

But trustees who are drawn to an institution's cause and by its culture are responsible for the long-term financial and programmatic well being of the institution. Generally speaking, the administration of the organization is primarily concerned with daily operations; it does not often have the luxury of contemplating the future.

Paradoxically, the board, which has that responsibility, may well find out that it will have to transform the institution to keep it healthy going into the future. That requires trustees to develop and oversee the implementation of strategies and policies to ensure the future viability of the institution in the always changing world in which it competes for students and money.

Any new strategies and policies required to respond to new external and internal forces will probably modify or recast the vision that attracted the individual board member in the first place. The ramifications of this are considerable. A trustee who finds him- or herself engaged in changing the very things that were initially attractive, at some cost in energy and time, may well decide not to do it. He or she may simply not exercise the responsibilities of the trust, or may lose interest. Neither is a desirable outcome for the school.

A better outcome would be one that encourages and supports the ethos of the organization, but that also encourages faculty and staff to support a slowly and carefully modified program that is more closely aligned with the market for the school's services and the environment in which it operates. This latter approach also has the advantage of focusing the trustee in an appropriate way on the school's long-term success.

Trustee Authority

In practice, boards tend to deal obsessively with easily grasped but irrelevant details and avoid major areas that require clear analysis and significant decision making. Very few people, including those on boards of trustees, want to be truly accountable and responsible, although major decisions require such responsibility and it is placed with the board.

Trustees' conduct is governed by statute, the organization's articles of incorporation or charter, by-laws and common law as well as written and unwritten policies and procedures. This authority to act is given to the board as a whole, of course, and not to individual members. This reality is often forgotten, to the detriment of the school.

Courts have recognized the authority of trustees to eliminate departments, approve cost-reduction programs, determine admissions standards, and increase or decrease salaries. Trustees have duties of care, loyalty and obedience to the corporation as a whole, and must perform their duties in good faith, in a manner they reasonably believe to be in the best interests of the corporation, and with such diligence, care and skill as ordinary prudent people would use under similar circumstances.

> To properly discharge the duty requires the active involvement in establishing corporate policies and direction and obtaining information to determine whether those policies and direction are being carried out.[3]

The board is responsible both for supervising asset utilization for corporate purposes and for preserving and maximizing assets. Its members are generally not liable for honest errors, but may be liable for breach of fiduciary duty, negligence, breach of contract or intentional misconduct. Hence it is usually bad practice, though not uncommon, for board members to be vendors to the school (e.g. insurance agents, investment brokers or attorneys). It is impossible in such a case to maintain the perception or actuality of a lack of conflict of interest between the trustee's role as vendor and the requirement imposed by the trustee's fiduciary duty to the school.

It is critical to note, though easy for boards to forget, that the quality of education parents purchase has a time-related component; it is not enough that things are going well this year, parents must also be confident that their children will enjoy a consistent level of quality for the duration of their attendance at the school. That will only happen if the board truly takes the long view of its responsibility as stewards for the financial, physical and human assets of the institution.

Board Organization

The board as a whole cannot, as a practical matter, do the evaluation and analysis necessary to assure itself that it is meeting its fiduciary responsibilities, so it creates committees to do that work. The committees then report regularly to the full board on their progress and bring to the board matters that require the deliberation and decision of the board as a whole, generally issues of policy.

Standing committees are those established by the institution's by-laws to oversee specific major areas of the school on behalf of the board as a whole. Boards should create as few standing committees as possible, and form ad hoc committees for specific, time limited, tasks. This helps to keep the entire board involved in the governance of the school. Standing committees generally include finance, facilities, development and trustees or governance. Good contemporary practice establishes an audit committee in order to better review and oversee financial/accounting practices and procedures to make sure they accurately reflect the operations of the school. Another committee should address compensation procedures and documentation, primarily but not only of the head of school. Both of these committees have very narrow but important responsibilities.

The executive committee is authorized to act for the board between regular board meetings or in an emergency. It should also be the planning committee of the board, charged with oversight of long-term planning as well as the annual agenda of the board.

The board president will establish ad hoc committees from time to time. Every board, for example, will eventually appoint a committee to search for a new head of school. Many boards establish committees to oversee major construction activity or to prepare a long-term facilities plan or to spearhead a capital campaign. Committees, standing or ad hoc, receive their legitimacy from the by-laws of the organization where the purpose of each standing committee is established and the conditions under which an ad hoc committee is established are spelled out.

It is important that ad hoc committees have a clear mandate, a defined life and a transparent process. If they do not, these committees may take on a life of their own and a level of influence that undercuts the board. These "rogue" committees may be called any number of innocent names, but they are distinguished by three characteristics: they are not provided for in the by-laws; they deal with important issues; and there are often no minutes.

If a committee is established to deal with the head's compensation, for example, and that committee continues to meet and discuss other central issues of the school, there may not be much left for the full board to deal with; in effect, a two level board is created, the appointed shadow board that deals with major issues, and the elected board that hears reports and goes home. Pretty soon members on the shadow board may begin to act independently from the rest of the board, and other real board members may get frustrated and stop attending meetings, resign, or start an internal battle to regain control. The potential damage of such unofficial ad hoc committees is very great and should be avoided.

Board committees should have a regular predicable and posted meeting schedule, agendas should be established and published, and minutes should be kept and distributed. Most board committees operate on an annual cycle and it should be possible to create an annual calendar of central agenda items. If a committee is expected to discuss a specific subject, any materials bearing on the subject should be distributed and reviewed by members prior to the meeting so that trustees can use their time productively during the meeting. This should be a trivial and obvious point but is far more honored in the breach than in the observance!

Board Meetings

Meetings of the board should follow the same procedures as those of board committees. That is, the agenda should be published in advance of the meeting with materials germane to the meeting distributed ahead of time. While the board will necessarily hear committee reports, it should hear those reports when the committees have something of substance to report, particularly when the report contains analysis and recommendations for board action. If there is nothing to discuss or act upon, the report of the committee should be made in writing and distributed to the board with the agenda and other material. Board meetings must be substantive if the board is to attract and retain competent, interested and active board members.

Evaluation of the Board

The NAIS *Trustee Handbook* includes only one reference to board evaluation as part of the responsibility of the committee on trustees[4] It does not address either the criteria necessary for such assessment (it directs readers to the NAIS web site) or the clear and measurable goals that should form the basis for such an assessment. One might infer from other material in the Handbook that since a trustee "actively supports and promotes the school's mission,"[5] is "accountable for the financial well-being of the school"[6] and "assures compliance with applicable laws and regulations"[7] specific criteria could be established and measured. But there is hard work here. First, the board must be knowledgeable and establish specific policies in its areas of accountability. It must then establish ways to measure the extent to which those policies have been implemented. It must then actually schedule regular time at meetings to accept reports and evaluate the success of the implementation.

Most boards now have a "committee on trustees" that is historically responsible for identifying and nominating new trustees, but is also responsible for evaluating how well the board really works. It is a critical responsibility. The success of the board is necessary for the long-term success of the school. Success requires, as discussed throughout, the same essential measurements as the rest of the organization: how well does the school carry out its mission and how well does that mission meet the needs and expectations of the school's constituencies. Trustees seldom think about their role literally, as preserving a "trust." But that is truly their responsibility and their reward; the support of a trust for the future (and the present) is worthy of their efforts.

It is useful to think of trustees, in the exercise of their trust, as one of four primary power centers in the organizations. The faculty, administration, and parents (particularly in day schools) are the others. They operate in an environment in which they interact and vie with one another to influence the resources and direction of the institution. At the same time they also have to pay attention to the demands and desires of secondary constituencies with interests in the institution – students, graduates, perhaps community groups – all of whom may wish to influence or at least to affect the school's operation and future.

The administration and faculty want to and do exercise authority over day-to-day implementation of the mission. In a sense, a properly focused board spends only part of its time overseeing current implementation of its policies. Most of its time is spent envisioning the future in which the school will operate and generating policies that will steer the organization successfully into that future. Conflict arises when the board spends too much time in the present and the administration and faculty try to effectively make policy that will affect the future. That turns governance on its head.

In *Governance as Leadership*[8] the authors identify three types of leadership; type I is fiduciary (oversight), type II is strategic (the future), and type III is what they call "generative."

> Generative thinking is essential to governing. As long as governing means what most people think it means — setting the goals and direction of an organization and holding management accountable for progress towards those goals, then generative thinking has to be essential to governing.[9]

The authors worry, as do others, that "boards have increasingly practiced a managerial version of governance. Instead of identifying problems, framing issues, or making sense of the organization, most boards address the problems that managers present to them."[10]

> But how can boards change; how can they suspend what they have thought were the rules under which they operate?
>
> Type III deliberation demands everything most board protocols discourage and trustees often dread. Many of us have been socialized to rely on rational discourse in the workplace. To 'think like a manager' means to think rationally. And because governing has increasingly been seen as a managerial activity, focused on Type I and Type II work, to think like a trustee also means to think like a manger.[11]

The kind of deliberation suggested is quite the opposite of the approach of most boards (the administration proposes, the board disposes). It requires trustees to do in their board role what most of them do in their own organizations: accept ambiguity and the lack of full information for decisions, accept that nonprofit organizations are not by nature rational, and be open to new understandings about the possibilities for the future.

Refocusing Board Priorities

But if boards are not thinking about the possibilities of the future (both anecdotal evidence and studies suggest they are not), the question to ask is how can a board become refocused and reenergized to accept its trust? The enabling conditions are straightforward.

- It cannot be done by fiat. The board president and a critical number of board members must be dissatisfied with the board's performance.

- There must be recognition at least by that group and by other critical constituencies that the work of the board is examination of and improvement in the ability of the board to carry out its responsibilities. This is not a weakness but a necessary and central part of the board's work.

- The physical operation of the board – its meeting structure, nominating process and committee operation – must change to encourage active and thoughtful participation during meetings which lead to actions or further targeted and measurable actions or activities. In other words, the operation of the board must be managed so that members feel their time and energy are being respected.

- An atmosphere must be created in which asking questions and evaluating ambiguous information is not only acceptable but is actively solicited and supported.

This is not a short process; it will take a long time. In fact, a well-managed board will regularly ask itself directly about its processes and goals and be sensitive to the feeling of commitment of its members.

That change is usually instituted by doing what an effective board is supposed to do: ask questions about the mission of the school and the role of the board in holding the administration accountable for the implementation of that mission; ask about how the board is evaluating the mission for its applicability to the future environment into which it will carry the organization; ask questions about board processes; and ask questions about board self-assessment.

Not all boards can be refocused. If the board is not working well and cannot be fixed, constituents should take that as a sign to transfer their energies and goals elsewhere.

Grappling with an Ineffective Board

I have raised a lot of issues that, taken together, suggest that most boards are not effective. If you are part of such a board, or have to work with such a board, you have no doubt thought about how an ineffective board can become effective. I believe that it can happen, but it is not easy. There are three primary conditions that must be met if there is any real hope to transform the board:

- There must be a general agreement that the board is not effective—and that its ineffectiveness is harming or will harm the school.

- Members of the board and of the school community must be willing not only to accept change but to make the decisions that will result in change.

- The composition of the board will probably have to change, especially if, as in many schools, boards are primarily or entirely parents of current students. This change may be inevitable and affected by the time period represented by their children's years of attendance. That is not to say that individuals cannot have another set of goals unrelated to their children, but it would take a conscious decision and special focus to carry off. It will also take time.

Boards can be ineffective without most constituencies knowing it. Schools, like most nonprofits, may seem to be doing well, especially to those who are used to how things work at the school and who support what they believe to be the mission and culture of the organization. Active parents will have figured out how to get things done for their children and will generally be satisfied if their children are happy and doing well academically. They will create, in effect, a little school that suits their values and goals within the larger school. So long as their little school satisfies them, they don't really see or care about the institution as a whole.

While schools do go out of business, it is usually the result of an economic or social change that may affect enrollment so slowly that the trends are not seen or are ignored. That is, a school may fail, but the failure is usually not precipitous, it happens over a period of time. Pure economic failure may also be hidden through increased fundraising for a time.

Clearly, if enrollment goals are widely missed, or accounts receivable increase radically, or if significant numbers of students are withdrawn to go to other independent schools or public schools, that should capture the attention of even very passive boards (unless the data are withheld by the head of school, which also happens). But most boards will not know if enrollment numbers are maintained by accepting less able students and even astute boards may not understand a slow change in demographics that will ultimately threaten the traditional base of the school. Moreover, my experience is that boards don't want to spend the time and energy required to really understand the demographics and economics of the environment in which they operate. Sometimes the failure to make strategic changes before trouble becomes obvious is itself a decision not to deal with a potential problem.

In order to reach agreement that the ineffective board, by not seeing or making appropriate critical decisions, needs to change, there must be some number of individuals, usually board members or parents and administrators who are respected members of the community who see clearly and can communicate persuasively. The need is not to criticize the board or its members, but more productively to articulate a case for changes that will enhance what most constituents believe attracted them to the institution in the first place. In other words, those who believe that the board is not effective need to focus on what is good and might be enhanced or improved, instead of focusing on what it believes to be bad. That is good psychology and good leadership.

Attacking current board members will not gain them sympathy (unless they are truly taking the school into bankruptcy).

None of this is to suggest that board members set out to be ineffective. Examples of effective and competent boards in both nonprofits and for-profit corporations would suggest that the role of trustees, and the role of corporate directors, is not well understood partly, I think, due to the short term thinking that this country is so familiar with. We are fixed on today and tomorrow; next year, or ten years from now, is not something on which we are trained to focus. Yet that is exactly what is required of trustees.

---

[1] Holland & Hester, Eds. *Building Effective Boards for Religious Organizations.* San Francisco: Josey-Bass, 2000.

[2] Chait, Richard P. et. al. *Governance as Leadership.* Hoboken, NJ: John Wiley & Sons, 2005.

[3] Ormstedt, David E. *Holding the Trust.* Washington, DC: National Association of Independent Schools, 2006.

[4] DeKuyper, Mary Hundley. *Trustee Handbook: A Guide to Effective Governance for Independent School Boards, Ninth Edition.* Washington, DC: National Association of Independent Schools, 2007.

[5] *Ibid*, p. 10

[6] *Ibid*, p. 10

[7] Ibid, p. 8

[8] Chait, Richard P. et. al. *Governance as Leadership.* Hoboken, NJ: John Wiley & Sons, 2005.

[9] *Ibid*, p. 89

[10] *Ibid*, p. 92

[11] *Ibid*, p. 120

Chapter 2

School Organization: The Administration

Given the fragmenting education marketplace and the rapidly growing though unclear influence of technology, what are the organizing principles boards of trustees should look to in the exercise of their fiduciary responsibility?

Schools should be organized in a way that maximizes flexibility, collaboration and communication. Administrative roles can be described by a two-axis framework, function and orientation. "Orientation," in this sense, refers both to the primary institutional function of the administrative department and also to the constituencies with which it primarily interacts. Schools, and the administrative areas therein, have both internal and external orientations.

In the following organization chart, each administrative area is grouped by orientation and includes the appropriate professionals who report to an administrator. Fundraising, Public Relations and Enrollment are oriented externally. Student Life and Academics are oriented internally. Finance & Administration supports the entire organization and is therefore oriented in both directions. In a large enough organization there may also be group administrators (i.e. assistant heads for Student Affairs and Marketing).

The area administrators (shaded) serve, with the head, as the school's executive committee and planning group. They provide a coordinative role in policymaking and policy dissemination and, with the experience of and feedback from their specialists, act as an effective advisory board to the head (and with the head, to the board of trustees). This coordinative function is repeated within each program area by a committee from within the area (Student Life, Academics, Fundraising, Public Relations, Enrollment, and Finance/Administration).

The school structure is usually duplicated at the board level. There are standing committees of the board for each of the areas represented on the planning committee. (In the following example, six domains are shown.) Those board committees have as their role advising the board on policy and providing oversight on behalf of the board to their corresponding administrative area.

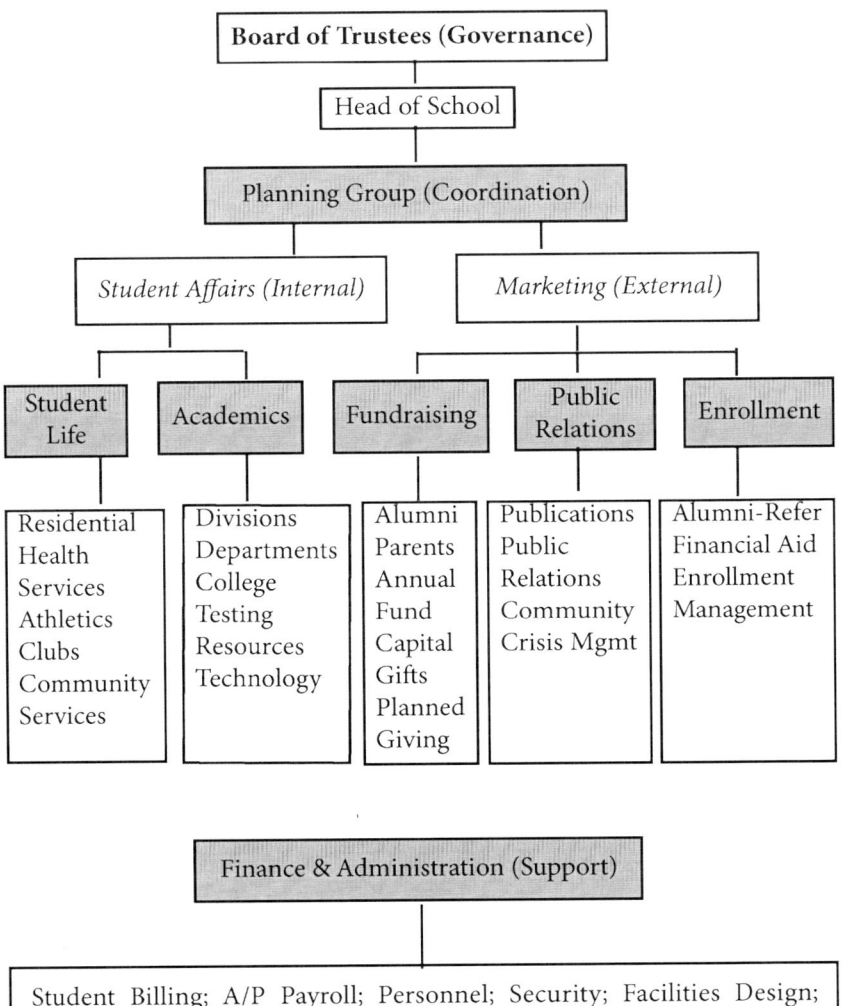

There are two competing tendencies in organizations: specialization and cooperation. Specialists are organized in vertical groups by specialty: teachers report to their department heads who report to their dean, buildings and grounds crews report to their supervisor who reports to the facilities director or business manager, and so on. But how are decisions made that require specialists from more than one group? In a traditional flat organization the baseball coach may need the field lined, but the groundskeepers have priorities assigned by the superintendent of buildings and grounds. Does the coach go to the head of school and the head direct the superintendent of buildings and grounds to then direct the groundskeepers to line the field? Does the head spend all afternoon consulting with all affected parties to make this happen? Unfortunately that is sometimes the case.

A much more practicable organizational model provides that much of the work of both the school and its board should be done not within the vertical domains, but rather in ad hoc groups based on required tasks. People generally are administered by specialty, but work more efficiently by task. That way flexibility is built in because groups will bring appropriate resources to bear on problems as they arise, then break up and recombine with whatever resources are required by the next problem or opportunity.

For example, a study of the use of financial aid as an enrollment tool would include an ad hoc group with members from academics, public relations, enrollment and finance. It might include trustees from the appropriate board committees. When recommendations work their way up through the planning committee to the head and board, there would then be consensus at the school level and enough knowledgeable trustees to support an informed discussion and policy decision at the board level.

While inclusion in an ad hoc planning group of the student life and academic areas is obvious enough, the recognition of areas to be included in an ad hoc group for the development of a marketing plan (communications, public relations, media relations, publications, development, and admissions) results from the need of a school to be clear in all its manifestations about how it presents itself. The reasons why parents send their children to private schools are many, but it is clear that the perception of a school is shaped by every element of that school. How it looks, the attitude of students during tours, the professional qualifications of staff, the look of its publications and its reputation with its graduates all make a difference.

The goal of the marketing plan is to tell the school's story to graduates, interested friends, community members, parents and potential students. The reputation of a school *is the school* in the perception of external constituencies. The development and communication of its image supports both admissions and fund-raising. Thus, while the areas may have functional operational differences, it does not make sense to organize these areas in a way that keeps them independent of each other when they are in fact interdependent.

In an organization with ad hoc task forces enabling flexibility, coordination and communication, the buildings and grounds staff, for example, work on priorities established by a group that includes the athletic director, the business manager, division heads, parents and other "users" of these services, so that the services can be efficiently allocated among competing demands. If that group is not making decisions that are consistent with the overall goals and objectives of the school, the senior planning group will evaluate the problem, analyze the adequacy of resources against the overall resource needs and recommend solutions to the head.

As this structure replaces the isolating vertical model of many independent schools, the role of the head of school will be re-defined. Leadership and management are often contrasted. The leader is supposed to encourage the moral and ethical reformation of the organization and engender the enthusiastic commitment of its employees and those in its expanded community to a common goal. Management, in turn, presumably makes sure the details in support of the school's goal articulated by the leader are thriftily accomplished.

In this organization, though, these roles are subsumed in another in which the head has some characteristics that are like those of a prime minister, a first among equals. The president of the board has a similar role. Each leader's job is to interpret the mission of the school in the light of current reality and to make sure that the resources available to them are properly allocated, according to how well they support the mission. The executive committee of the board or the full board is the means by which policy is made and the planning group of the administration is the means by which implementation of those policies is effected.

Because employees of this organization are presumed to be specialists and know their jobs, once policies are established with due process and collaboration, operational decisions are made, with a full hearing of the various alternatives communicated through the planning group, on the one hand, and the project (committee) leaders on the other. Decisions will be implemented because they are made on the basis of wide knowledge and involvement.

The function of the head, acting on the policy direction of the board, is to hire, facilitate and evaluate the members of the planning group and the results of the group's efforts.

The old organizational model served schools well in simpler times. Now, neither students nor faculty nor trustees are satisfied to participate in a one-way relationship. The organization itself, dealing with new and often unstable student families, new demands from regulators and government, a much higher than traditional exposure to litigation from all constituents, and the effects of technology, is pulled in so many directions that any head or board president who expects to have all information flow to and all decisions made by him or her (as the only one who has, supposedly, all the relevant information) will quickly be pulled apart. A very strong leader may still be able to hold the organization together, but centrifugal action will tear it apart at the least sign of instability at the center. In the new model, the leaders have willing followers who, because of their involvement in and subsequent ownership of organizational decisions, help the head and president to shape the institution for success. Communication and collaboration are built into the organizational structure and the energy of the organization is used to develop, assess and implement mission, rather than coerce support for unilateral decisions.

Paradoxically, such an organization may well recognize that the traditional educational functions it is organized to support may best be decentralized, perhaps into the outside community. I think that will happen, and it will put even more of a premium on equal involvement of skilled collaborators in a mutually supportive environment. The more dispersed the functions this group supports and supervises, the greater the premium on communications and collaboration, because the pieces and parts become more complex and diffuse and no one individual can manage the whole. Students and faculty may be working sometimes in the same space, which may be the school facility or somewhere half way around the world. They may be working in separate spaces synchronously or asynchronously, in communication through email, instant messaging, interactive web access or some other way.

Management of the logistics of such a school will test any management team, but it may also be enormously exciting, and it may allow and support a learning environment perfectly tuned to the needs, interests and capabilities of its students and their families. And that is the real reward for trustees who understand and willingly accept the gift of the trust they have been given.

Chapter 3

The Head of School and the Board

The relationship between the head and the board defines the nature of the institution and absolutely affects its long-term success.

In many schools, once the new head has been appointed, the board retires, expecting that it will be informed of major initiatives and made aware of issues and events that may require a response to parents or concerned neighbors. The board may be consulted, usually in the form of discussions between the head and the board president. The expectation (and often the reality in many schools) is that once hired, the head provides vision, leadership and direction. Some boards specifically reinforce that unhealthy relationship, sometimes expressed as "the administration proposes, the board disposes." That not only misunderstands the role of the board but also puts responsibilities in the wrong place.

It is the basic premise of these chapters that the board holds the vision and hires a head to implement that vision. Where that is not the case, schools tend to change direction each time a new head is hired. That is disruptive and destabilizing, especially because the average head lasts only slightly longer than the average board member.

The relationship between the head and the board is dynamic because implementation activities will probably, in the day-to-day reality of running a school, affect the vision over time as the environment changes. Recognizing that the vision is a living thing that may be modified even while it is being realized, the board must nevertheless keep its hold on the vision and make sure that the head does not have a very diff
erent idea about what the school ought to be doing. When they are not working on the same vision, the board and head will be going in different directions, which usually results in the head being forced out. The resulting problems for the school are squarely the responsibility of the board.

In a discussion about financing facilities construction and renovation, the head of School A explained his philosophy clearly to his guests from School B: to improve and enhance facilities through debt financing as rapidly as possible. This would allow his school to become more selective and to attract a parent body that could pay the cost of the increasing debt. His plan was to secure the future of his school not through endowment but enrollment. Because it would become a first tier school of choice, enrollment would not be affected by an economic downturn. His board president beamed at him throughout this exposition.

The head and members of the board of School B listened carefully because they had major facilities needs. They thanked their host cordially. The strategy of the first school, however, was not an option for the second because the second school's vision was to work with students who were precisely not the kind of kids that the first school wanted. It would not change that vision in order to build buildings. The second school needed to improve its facilities, but also needed the security of an endowment because its enrollment probably would be affected by an economic slowdown.

These are two very different (and real) visions. What would happen to the second school if the board hired a new head whose aspirations mirrored the head of the first school? If the transition were successful, which is unlikely, it would be an entirely different school, not the one envisioned by those who first entrusted it to the board.

Transitions, however, can and do happen. To be successful, the need for change must be rooted in the accepted historical vision of the school and the reasons for the change must be clear and persuasive. Change is usually necessary when the environment in which the original trust was created changes. In that case the objectives of the trust might no longer be valid. Then it would be the duty of the board to reformulate the objectives and effectuate necessary changes to reach those objectives.

The job of the head of school varies with the needs of the school, with the relative power of the faculty and trustees, and with the personality of the incumbent. Responsible to the board, the head is the operational authority in all areas in which he or she takes an interest and in which other, more powerful constituents do not. That is to say that in these complicated days, the independent authority of the head is in practice substantially limited by his or her constituents, either because of their persuasive power, financial power or their power to disrupt the operation of the school by requiring enormous amounts of the head's time and energy. Responsible for the safety, security and college pretensions of students, for the changing needs and expectations of their parents, and for the security and fragile egos of the faculty, the job is increasingly difficult. Those heads who served 20 or more years have mainly been forced out, are retired or have died in office. It is highly unlikely that there will be many heads of school with 20 years tenure again.

Heads operate with two structural problems: in this age of instant communication the expectations for instant gratification are far more insistent than they once were, and there is no clear and explicit accountability against which to measure success (or failure).

Without clearly defined and supported measurable outcomes, success exists only so long as people believe in it. "Hot" schools are hot because parents and their children think they are hot. When they stop thinking so, the school is no longer hot. Nothing may have changed; faculty and curriculum and facilities may all be the same. But the belief system has changed, and therefore the perception has changed. There is nothing that the board or the administration or faculty can do about that perception except to be aware of it and, if it is deemed to be important, to try to feed it. That may be enormously time-consuming and will probably fail. Managing perception is harder than managing reality.

The head needs the support and counsel of the board and its president to do the job. It is a partnership with different responsibilities and powers, but they are, unfortunately, generally undefined, and thus give rise to issues and tensions that affect the entire institution.

The NAIS *Trustee Handbook* states it this way:

> As the chair of the board, you understand that there is no more important factor in the success of the school than the relationship of chair and head of school. You make central to your beliefs and actions the knowledge that together those partners share – and model – leadership and governance and determine all that follows. [1]

There is no question that the relationship is critical and important. The head and board president must work closely together, but no individual board member can act for the board as a whole. The leadership required of the head of school is derived from and subject to the understanding of the board of the requirements of its trust. The head is an instrument of the board, critical to its responsibility but nevertheless subservient to their understanding of their responsibility. When a head makes decisions that are not consistent with the board's understanding of the members' trust, the board must require corrective action. This is usually communicated by the president directly to the head; it is not the will of the president that is being communicated but of the board as a whole. In this sense, the relationship of the president and head makes possible effective communication between the board and the head. Board presidents and heads sometimes confuse the message with the messenger, to the detriment of the board and the institution.

This relationship can fail in two ways: there may be no communication and the head goes without direction or control, or the board president may communicate his or her agenda, not that of the board as a whole. In either case the will of the board is severed from the stewardship of the institution, and that may affect the future success of the organization and the willingness of effective people to serve on the board. Neither outcome is good.

The head must lead the school and make decisions in the course of that leadership. Unfortunately, there is seldom a clear and unambiguous choice between a "good" decision and a "bad" decision. More often, there are choices among a number of "good" decisions. The relationship of the head and board president is especially important because the quality of leadership that builds excellent schools or other institutions is not necessarily rational or objective. While there may be clear objectives and accountabilities, there may also be no right answers – only different answers with varying implications and results—for the school and for the community.

The relationship is further complicated for heads who have grown up in faculty meetings or heads who, no matter how natively authoritarian, have made themselves believe in expressions of consensus and power sharing with faculty or staff. They may substitute the language of process for process itself. Or they may believe that they need to make decisions, even if that jeopardizes desired goals, so that their constituents will see that the head does not lack authority independent of the board. In either case, a head may avoid one trap only to fall into another, which is to move separately from the board and thus lose its support. Board support of the head cannot exist without good and honest communications.

Schools need a head who is a person of character, who is interested in the job because he or she thinks that schools are important places, who has a clear, unambiguous view of what the school can be consistent with the board's vision and the environment in which it operates, and who knows how to get there. Reality dictates that the candidate must also be a true delegator. That means an individual who is confident enough in his or her own capabilities and in the support of the board to allow subordinates to make mistakes. That means an individual who can make mistakes without ego crashes. The head should be someone who recognizes what needs to be done but knowing that it cannot all be done, chooses goals and objectives that are clear, unambiguous and manageable. The head also needs to be secure enough to be able to share the venture with the board, particularly the board president.

The board president should also be a person of character who is interested in the job because he or she thinks that schools are important places, who has a clear vision of what the school can be consistent with the vision of the board as a whole and the environment in which it operates, and who knows how to hire and support the head to help it get there. The president also needs to be someone whose ego allows her or him to play a lead role, but one that does not interfere with the need of the head to be the school's leader. It is a position of great power and influence, but it is generally not a position in the public spotlight. It is, in short, a sort of thankless job, whose satisfaction comes from laying out the course and applauding the contestants, but lacks the satisfaction of running or winning the race.

Both the head and the president must understand that their responsibilities will be interdependent. If the board dominates, the head's leadership will be impaired which inevitably threatens the institution. If the head dominates, there will be no effective board constraints and little requirement to build for the future. In a sense, in good head/president relationships power sharing is divided temporally – the head in the present and the board in the future. There is overlap, of course. The present is not static and the future quickly becomes and is influenced by the present. But it is precisely this division of focus that allows the partnership to operate for the benefit of the institution.

Because of the partnership, both the head and the president can and should inspire and support their followers – faculty, staff and students for the head, active and engaged board members for the president and parents and other external constituencies for both. It is too easy to focus on problems and ignore things that work. The effective leader recognizes where his or her energy needs to go and is unafraid to cut loose those that do not want to be there. The head and board president in partnership are clear about boundaries and therefore willing to take the risks that are inherent in guiding their schools.

Hiring a New Head of School

"Because hiring the head is the single most important action the board can undertake, it should be done carefully, procedurally and not too frequently."[2] I would suggest that it is undoubtedly a very important job but the board has other equally important responsibilities. If the board has made sure that there are clear goals and policies to support them, and a strong and committed staff, the choice of a particular head of school is not such an "important action."

After all, schools experience changes of head very frequently. If the school is overly "head-centric" the chances of whiplash to the vision and mission of the organization are very strong. The head is certainly important, but mostly if he or she has a special talent that will help the school move to a new level or as an agent for a specific goal (build a new building, ramrod a capital campaign, map the curriculum).

And if a high quality search were the most important action of boards, based on the turnover statistics, it cannot be said they do it very well.

[1] DeKuyper, Mary Hundley. *Trustee Handbook: A Guide to Effective Governance for Independent School Boards, Ninth Edition.* Washington, DC: National Association of Independent Schools, 2007, p. 145.
[2] *Ibid*, p. 128

Chapter 4

The Role of the Chief Financial Officer

The Complicated Dynamic

This book is primarily a discussion of trustees and their responsibilities, one of which is a close working relationship with the CEO of the organization, the head of school. However, there is another administrator whose relationship to the board and board president is also critical. That administrator is the chief financial officer or CFO of the school.

The CFO is responsible for most of the support services of the organization, including accounts payable and receivable, payroll, benefits management, and facilities and administrative services. The CFO works closely with the head to develop the annual budget for the school and monitors expenditures against that budget.

Because so much of the work of the board has financial implications the CFO is very involved with committees of the board as well as individual board members, especially the president, the treasurer and the chair of the facilities committee. The CFO does the projections and budgets for initiatives being considered by the board.

Because of the dual relationship with the head of school and the board, the CFO plays a complicated role. Board members need to understand that dynamic.

While schools often used to fill the job of business officer with a teacher who was tired of teaching, these positions are increasingly being filled by mid-career professionals with business training. This trend suggests that school heads and school boards realize that institutions have become complicated businesses and that the complexities now require a higher level of business experience and skills.

Because heads hire professional CFOs does not mean that they understand or want to understand the complexities of the business. This may create a certain tension between the CEO and the CFO: the head's natural focus is on delivery of program, often without consideration of the cost of people and material while the CFO is focused on those costs, often with substantial pressure from the treasurer of the board and the finance committee.

In addition, heads of school inevitably have been teachers not corporate managers, and tend to value flexibility, believe in management by consensus and want to support creativity. A CFO has little tolerance for open ended flexibility. He or she needs clear decisions and fairly tight management so that income and expenses are in balance.

It is also often the case that members of the board, perhaps including the board president or some other strong trustee, are essentially fundraisers rather than managers. This may lead them to try to manage the appearance of the information to suit their fundraising purpose rather than to reflect the substance of the figures and their implication for the health of the institution. This puts the CFO in a very difficult position.

CFOs should and usually do feel that they have a fiduciary responsibility to safeguard the assets of their institutions. The board should understand (and wise ones do) that the roles of the head and CFO are, in a sense, structurally in conflict with no neutral power to adjudicate. In fact, in this potential conflict, there is precisely no disinterested party.

When CFOs are asked what irritates them about heads, they inevitably mention heads making decisions that affect budgets without consulting them, micromanaging, and lack of communication. Heads, on the other hand, see CFOs as not willing to spend money when needed for program and as more concerned with budget than education. Nervous jokes about tightwad CFOs are common among heads.

In well run schools heads and CFOs are collaborators who divide the operation of the school instinctively and, with good communications, deliberately. They are partners and see themselves as such. While they may not always agree (and their daily responsibilities are truly different), they understand the basis for their disagreement and are able to negotiate a resolution to the conflict. Boards should be alert to the potential for members to exploit this dynamic for purposes of furthering their own individual agendas. Trustees can and do try to play the head against the CFO to support their goals. The best way for board presidents to avoid this exploitation is to keep the board focused and collaborative so that agendas are formulated within and by the board as a whole.

If they are experienced and thoughtful, boards and heads also understand that in a community of teachers the hand that holds the purse strings belongs to a figure of authority, a person who can and often should say "no." Faculty often do not want to deal either with authority or with permission or with "business." So CFOs represent, in a sense, a threat to their self-confidence, to their self-image. School faculties may try to wall off the CFO (or even the head if perceived to have similar tendencies), and they can be remarkably skillful in doing just that.

At the same time, the board of trustees is made up of a variety of people with different agendas and needs. They are in their roles because they have ties to the school, generally as parents or graduates. While their agendas may be different, they are united in defending their idea of what makes the school special to them and very seldom will think of it as a business. This is all the more remarkable because membership on a school board usually involves a financial commitment to the school and members who make that commitment can do so because they are themselves successful business or professional people. The CFO, hired to attend to just those business dimensions of the institution, is in the strange position of being suspect if he or she is aggressive, or someone to be co-opted to protect some parochial interest. Striking the right balance in a complicated setting is difficult. Board members, led by the president of the board, should be clear about how they perceive the role of the CFO as he or she provides staff support to the board, and particularly how they expect the relationship of the CFO and head to work.

In practice, CFOs who cannot work out an operating relationship that supports both program and the imperatives of the business demands of the schools in which they work tend to find jobs elsewhere because the demand is high. There is always a cost of that change, however, to the school as well as to the CFO.

The wise CFO also has a role with the directors of Development and Admissions. These relationships arise because the CFO, focused on keeping the bills paid and facilities maintained during the current academic year, will also have an interest in the continuation of the enterprise in the future.

Admissions represents, in a practical sense, the perceived success of the institution on the street; it is a pretty good measure of how customers feel about the product. If there is strong and steady interest in the school, demonstrated by steady or growing inquiries and applications, and the yield (those who actually enroll as a percentage of all who apply) is steady or increasing, there will be a predictable and stable stream of income. A wise CFO (and responsible board member) will want to be cognizant of admissions trends. In a badly run school, admissions directors will not be happy about the CFO's interest.

The other income stream, from unrestricted donations (the annual fund) and from income earned on restricted gifts (endowment) is also of considerable interest to the CFO for the same reasons: predictable, stable and sufficient income streams.

Facilitator of a Collaborative Budget Process

The budget process is at the center of what a good CFO does. It should be of considerable interest to the board and, through its finance committee, should ensure that the process works in support of mission as well as for the immediate needs of the school. If the CFO can create and manage a process by which the planning for the school is done by means of collaborative budget making and management, the school will probably succeed. That may be somewhat presumptuous since it is the educational vision that defines a school. But budgets are planning documents, in the best sense; they are the common and visible language with which resources are allocated to educational program. Equally important, those involved in the process have an opportunity to understand and influence the priorities supported by the budget. A well-designed budget structure and open budget-building process level the playing field because all involved have a fair shot at acquiring the assets they require for their programs.

A collaborative budget process requires administrators and educators to understand each other and each other's responsibilities. It must also have a supportive board that ultimately must adopt the end result of the process as its own. While budgets provide a way for the administration to control expenditures, if the expenditures being controlled have been agreed to in a fair and open process, those who helped to create the budget will do the controlling; the CFO will not have to do it.

The real job of the CFO, therefore, is as a facilitator of the creation process and a reporter of how the school is doing relative to the agreed upon budget. Indeed, if the CFO needs to specifically manage expenditures, there is a major problem because that means that the budgeting process is not understood and supported, and people are operating in their own, not the school's interest.

Chapter 5

The Business of Education

A school offers health insurance to its employees. To keep costs down, a lower cost insurance program is introduced that has similar benefits but is somewhat less convenient than its current program. Senior faculty and administrators subscribe to the current expensive product and will not switch to the cheaper plan. The head, significantly, will not set an example. The cost of the high priced plan then increases by 40 percent, which throws the budget into deficit. In desperation the head freezes salaries.

As this is unfolding, the board fails to approve a spending plan that would limit endowment contribution to the operating fund. Because all endowment income has historically gone into the operating fund, the endowment has been losing its purchasing value at a rapid rate. (It is being decapitalized.) But because the budget was put together with the assumption that that the board would approve a reduced endowment contribution, the school actually ends the fiscal year with a huge surplus— which the board hides from the faculty. This is a true story!

The example above illustrates a pattern of behavior that combines failure of board oversight with a lack of professional management. This situation is not uncommon; there are six contributing causes:

1. Schools are in a **competitive marketplace**, which means that prices (tuition) may not be related to actual costs. This exacerbates problems of budget making and budget control because money may not be available for required staff and/or equipment. Even during cycles of high demand, fees that competing schools charge tend to be spread over a rather narrow range. The actual percent of educational costs supported by tuition, however, varies tremendously because both fixed and variable costs vary even within contiguous geographical areas. Schools allied with related institutions may, for example, spread some overhead costs over the various entities. School endowments and

annual giving resources also vary significantly. Those schools without a large endowment and/or a significant income from other sources, but with tuitions at the market level, will be hard pressed to support the same level and quality of services as their richer competitors.

2. Schools are also in a **commodity market** in which they compete in price only by type of school, with schools within comparable tiers pricing their services closely with each other to avoid price competition. Pricing is carefully calibrated to ensure that tuitions are not undercut (i.e., we can only charge for our type of school what we know parents will have to pay elsewhere).

There are certainly many parents and students who do respond to programmatic differentiation and make choices appropriate to the personalities and capabilities of each student. As in canned vegetables, some store brands are better than others and better than the "brand" name. Some consumers know that, but most are sensitive to price, assuming one can of peas is much like another. A few will always buy the brand name for the security or the prestige, whether it is peas, vodka or education, while the rest go where they can get in.

3. **Cost of production**, especially salaries, benefits and utilities, rise above the rate of inflation, further squeezing resources. There is a conventionally held notion that "our faculty should be paid in the top 10 percent of teachers in our market." Schools end up chasing their own and each other's tails. They are also chasing the union-driven teacher salaries of the public schools, which exacerbates the private schools' financial burden and the costs to parents. There are public school districts in which starting teachers' salaries are higher than independent schools' median salaries in the same area.

4. **Overhead** has grown in response to external challenges from regulators, internal pressure for equipment and instructional support, and from parents' demands for tangible exhibits of where their money goes. Major determinants of overhead are rising expectations for facilities and an increasing clarity about the cost of deferred maintenance; the complexity of the regulatory and municipal environments in which schools operate; and, from out of nowhere in the last few years, the cost of technology. Many schools have found that

from literally nothing, the cost of computers, software, support salaries, contracts, wiring and access costs are now perhaps three to four percent or more of total budgets. This does not replace any other cost; in fact, technology costs are probably understated because technology also affects other costs such as teacher training, furniture, fixtures and electricity.

5. **There is little tradition of professional management** of nonprofit organizations in general and schools in particular. While schools have increasingly turned to men and women from the corporate world for their business and facilities needs, there is no tradition of rigorous oversight of finance and facilities by trustees. Without clearly articulated and measurable goals, that tradition is unlikely to develop.

6. **Boards are inadequate** in preparation, education and understanding of their roles. Commentators have long bemoaned the proclivity of nonprofit board members to leave their objective business sense at the boardroom door. In the literature and in practice it is too often the head of school who assumes the responsibility to lead the board. In this regard, the National Association of Independent Schools and the various regional associations generally do not do a very good job in educating trustees, partly because that is neither their focus nor expertise (they are mostly managed by former heads of school) and partly because trustees tend not to believe that they need training.

Educators and trustees may understand many of these constraints, but that understanding does not generally lead to significant change. When asked how a certain, critical decision might be made, one head of school literally stated after some thought, *"We are not organized to make that kind of decision."* Rigorous development of problem definition and solution alternatives does not inform organizational or operational structures in most nonprofit organizations. The bottom line for most nonprofits is service, not profit. Therefore most are more focused on the construct of the service than on *how to deliver* the service (or, indeed, whether the service is the right service).

Evaluating Success

A serious problem for schools or other nonprofit institutions is how to evaluate success. A for-profit organization can look at its sales statistics, costs of goods sold, return on investment and net income to determine whether profits balance risk. A nonprofit relies ultimately on market share: if the audience drops, the applications fall, or the donations dry up, it is pretty clear that the organization has failed in its mission or has picked the wrong mission, one not supported by its constituencies. It is a question of the value perceived by those whom the organization is intended to benefit.

The real question is how a school can judge its success or failure before the development of an evident threat to its market share. The answer is to ask the right questions and then act on the answers! Schools, like any organization, need clear and measurable goals in support of a clearly articulated mission based on a broadly communicated and shared vision.

Competition in the real world drives down margins and drives out non-competitive organizations. Independent schools are not immune to those pressures. Beyond public schools there are various other institutions and practices that promise significant potential competition if they succeed. These include the rapidly growing home school movement and an increasing number of charter schools, which are public schools run by private nonprofit or for-profit organizations but supported largely by public dollars. "Distance Learning" is quickly growing in the corporate world and in higher education. There is a notion that it will work with adults but not with children. It is equally possible, however, that combining the World Wide Web with home schooling and the occasional use of public facilities may be a powerful alternative to expensive private education.

There are very few families today willing to spend $25 to $30 thousand (or more) above what they are already paying for school as part of their property taxes. While it is undeniable that a few (mostly boarding) schools do have that attraction and that there are a few specialty schools (largely those that cater to children with learning disabilities) that can command high (often state or city funded) tuitions, most non-religious private schools exist because acceptable, less expensive educational alternatives are not available. And while parents say overwhelmingly that the attraction of private schools is quality and small class size, they also state that their local public schools are poor.

The notion that many parents will spend what is for many of them most or all of any discretionary income on private schools simply for prestige when there are reasonable public alternatives is ludicrous. Both personal and professional experience suggests that the quality argument alone is specious. When money does not concern a family, there are a number of other criteria that become important. In a NAIS study several years ago[1], respondents from the population at large rated the following as important and then compared how well private schools embodied them as opposed to public schools:

	Private	Public
High quality teachers	47%	22%
Prevent drug & alcohol use	36%	17%
Motivate students about learning	41%	14%
Challenging students to do their best	46%	12%
Encouraging participation by parents	48%	14%
Maintain Discipline	63%	11%
Support a climate where success is okay	48%	10%

Parents who send their children to independent schools may or may not agree with that list, although presumably they would. But other characteristics might include social value, location (is it convenient to commuting routes to work?), hours and availability of before- and after-school programs, the school's success in placing children in desired colleges and universities, and the strength of athletic programs. The cost of independent schools is a concern and has ramifications that may not be adequately understood.

Where money is an issue, which is the case for the vast majority of people, the concern is more basic: is there a viable public alternative, one where there is reasonable academic rigor and one that is safe?

The Changing Marketplace

In the face of tight money and increasing competition, both from traditional competitors and from a new, profit-seeking educational-industrial sector, the need for better and more deliberate management should but does not appear to be self-evident.

The demographics of school-aged children are interesting and should raise some concerns for educators in both the public and private sectors. Actual and projected enrollments in thousands by NCES are:

Year	Public	Private
1990	41,217	5,234
2000	47,204	6,155
2010(p)	48,842	6,510
2014(p)	49,993	6,695

Within those numbers, which assume a continued percentage of private school enrollment at around 13 percent, there is significant variation. Members of the National Association for Independent Schools enrolled 561,679 students in 2006-2007, slightly less than one percent of school age children 3 to17 years old. That is up 33 percent over 10 years. Member schools of the Association totaled 1,025 or 4 percent of private schools. Catholic Schools numbered 8,353 or 30 percent of total private schools.

Publicly funded but privately run charter schools represent a new but significant element of education. The Center for Education Reform estimates that as of June, 2008 school year there were 4,225 charter schools serving 1,242,427 students. That is four times the number of traditional independent schools.

But 4,434,000 children were not enrolled in either public or private schools. While estimates vary wildly, the National Household Education Survey [NHES] from 2003 states that in the spring of 2003 1,096,000 students were being home schooled, a figure that represents a 29 percent increase from 1999. "In addition, the estimated home schooling rate—the percentage of the student population being home schooled—rose from 1.7 percent in 1999 to 2.2 percent in 2003."[2]

In 1996 and 1999 NHES asked parents their reasons for undertaking home schooling. Several themes emerge from these responses. First is the issue of educational quality. The parents of one-half the home schoolers in these surveys were motivated by the idea that home education is better education. A large share also viewed the issue in terms of shortcomings of regular schools: the parents of 30 percent of home schoolers felt the regular school had a poor learning environment, 14 percent objected to what the school taught, and another 11 percent felt their children weren't being challenged at school. Another theme had to do with religion and morality. Religion was cited by 33 percent of parents and morality by 9 percent. Practical considerations (transportation to school, the cost of private school) seemed of relatively minor importance. If attitudinal responses are to be believed, home schooling is not primarily a religious phenomenon, although religion is important. Further, families participating in home schooling do not cite educational cost as a barrier, even though one might presume that private schools could respond to their academic and moral concerns.[3]

In education, as in other areas of society, the population is fragmenting. And that suggests that the failure of board oversight and lack of professional management that characterize private school administration must change if these schools are to survive. Unless boards and administrators understand the changing nature of the marketplace and the rapid commoditization of education, learn to manage direct and overhead costs, and hire and support professional management, independent schools will face potentially fatal consequences.

The recognition that schools exist on the sufferance of their constituencies and that those constituencies have expectations they demand be met is new in education. It is both frightening and exhausting. Many if not most educators therefore ignore the power of those expectations. That is a mistake. It is not, as has been noted, the traditional "competitors" that will destroy a school but the new competitors that may not be schools at all in the traditional sense. They may be home schooling parents or users of distance learning on the Internet. The explosion of information and its easy availability are twin challenges that must be faced, understood and embraced in a direct and proactive way by school boards and administrators.

Diversity and Financial Aid

This is the constant topic at meetings, workshops and conventions. Those who can afford to pay the tuition at most schools (and, in the case of day schools, can afford to pay the tariff to live near them) tend to be wealthy and white.

The degree of wealth is the surprise. With the cost of big city independent schools at $25,000 to $30,000 and more, it takes $90,000 of annual gross income to pay the tuition and related bills for two children. With a median household income in 2007 of $5,740[4], it becomes clear that these schools are not filled with middle class children.

As our society becomes increasingly multi-cultural, schools spend a large and increasing amount of their tuition income to attract minority students sufficient to provide critical mass in each grade and section. Many of those minority families understand and play the system (in which some schools also participate); they can secure very large financial aid awards regardless of their income

Enrollment of students of color in independent U.S. schools has increased steadily in the last 20 years and was 20.8 percent in the 2007-2008 school year. It is highest on the west coast, where Asian-American students live in large numbers. Overall, Asian-American students were 6.5 percent and African-American students 5.9 percent of total enrollment. In the same year, 8.8 percent of administrators and 12.5 percents of teachers were people of color.[5]

For comparison, in 2003, all schools in the United Stated totaled 41.3 percent of the population was non-white. Of that total, 17.2 percent was black and 18.5 percent Hispanic. While diversity has long been a heavily subsidized goal of independent schools, they have only half of the racial diversity of public schools.

The argument for buying diversity has been so compelling to schools that many spend 12 to15 percent of their tuition income to do so. The cost is very significant, and not just in devalued revenue. The cost of recruiting students and faculty of color, the cost of processing financial aid applications, the cost of providing remedial help, testing and counseling is all drained from the need to educate the remaining 85 percent of the student body.

Although reasons for active recruitment of employees and students of color are seldom clearly articulated, the drive for diversity in schools has two main sources: the need for a public charity to contribute to its community in return for its tax-free status, and the idea for people being trained to live in an increasingly diverse and multi-cultural society, the culture and history of minority students enrich the educational program of the institution and benefit all students.

Building a diverse organization has additional benefits; it expands the pool in which employees and students can be found, it requires the school to manage its affairs and design its curriculum and community in a way that more accurately reflects the world in which it operates than would otherwise be the case. In addition, treating people of color seriously forces the organization to examine how open it is to diversity and how well it is prepared for that diversity. That examination may well discover practices no longer relevant to the mission of the school, or even detrimental to that mission.

The cost of education has, as noted above, generally driven both the majority and minority "middle class" out of independent schools, leaving the very wealthy and the very poor. Or to put it another way, redefining "middle class" well away from the median household income. While almost 11.6 percent of all school-age children attended non-public schools in 2005[6], 43 percent of those with incomes above $75,000 attend those schools.

Diversity in schools is far more important to the majority than to the minority — to the white and wealthy population who might otherwise have no direct experience of a society different from their own. A number of students of color have written about their experiences in independent schools with some anger. For minority students, attendance at a diverse school may be the only way to obtain the education they feel they need to have any economic opportunity, but that does not mean they prefer being minority participants in the school's culture.

In a pure market-driven organization there would be very little financial aid, because a lower tuition rate would be a major enrollment-enhancing tool. Schools that do not compete on tuition, however, can afford to appear to be diverse and support multi-cultural awareness on whatever grounds they choose.

This is an ongoing discussion, as it should be, but it is not usually a public discussion. Boards support diversity, but it is often unexamined support. It is difficult to question the virtue of helping inner city minority students escape an environment in which they may have no other opportunities. Of course, even in the attempt to be diverse there is no true diversity. Those minority students who are attracted to and succeed at private schools do so only if their value system is reasonably synchronized with that of the majority and if they are disciplined enough to put up with the majority culture. Diversity is truly economic in most schools. The more a minority student is rooted in a value system different from the majority, the more valuable that student would be to the school and the less likely that he or she would succeed in the school environment.

Boards are responsible for the school's policies about diversity and their responsibility is not simply to set an enrollment target. They need to make sure that once minority students arrive they are not left to sink or swim, as is often the case. Part of the cost of the push for diversity is to have in place academic and social structures that will, in so far as possible, make minority students feel welcome in the majority culture into which they have been recruited.

Boards must be clear about their support for diversity and need to clearly understand its true costs — economic, social, administrative and programmatic — as well as the benefits. The terms of discussion are heavily loaded and the conversation is likely to be uncomfortable. Because the idea and fact of diversity strikes so deeply into how schools operate, it is hard to see how boards cannot pay attention.

[1] *Public Perception of Quality Education.* Washington DC: National Association of Independent Schools, 1999.

[2] *"Homeschooling in the United States: 2003," Executive Summary,* Washington DC: National Center for Education Statistics, 2003.

[3] Bauman, Kurt J. *"Home Schooling in the United States: Trends and Characteristics."* Washongton DC: U.S. Census Bureau Working Paper, 2001.

[4] *American Community Survey.* Washington DC: U.S. Census Bureau, 2007.

[5] *Facts at a Glance for All Independent Member Schools, www.nais*.org

[6] National Center for Educational Statistics, nces.ed.gov/fastfacts

Chapter 6

Endowment Management

One of the primary jobs of the board is either directly or indirectly to supervise the investment of endowment funds, although as mentioned above, there is no tradition of rigorous oversight of finance and facilities by trustees. This is unfortunate because the endowment represents the capital of the organization, usually built from gifts intended by their donors to be permanently invested so that income from those investments can be used for either general or specifically restricted purposes by the school. These are funds held in trust on behalf of their donors. Since the budgets of most schools are highly dependent on tuition income, income from invested capital ("endowment") can provide a critical addition for such things as salaries, financial aid to needy families, support for plant maintenance or many other purposes. Schools, like other organizations, have more competing needs than they have resources. With the exception of a handful of truly wealthy schools with huge endowments and schools that have other kinds of resources, there is never enough money.

At one institution the administration had decided that it was critically important to the mission of the institution to keep tuition down. The business manager instructed the investment manager, therefore, to invest all funds (which were substantial) in fixed income securities with the highest current income. He then took all of that income to support the operating budget.

Subsequently a review of the endowment was undertaken, which showed that while a $10 million endowment had over 15 years become $20 million, in current dollars (reflecting the actual purchasing power of the investment) it was worth $7 million. Since all of the income had been taken out, the endowment had not been allowed to grow enough at least to keep up with inflation and therefore had declined in real terms. This is called "decapitalization," which pretty well describes the process.

Confronted with decapitalization of its endowment, the finance committee of the board and the board chair nevertheless were unwilling to address the question of asset allocation. It took a change in investment managers and a number of presentations by investment analysts before the board could be convinced to accept its fiduciary and legal responsibilities to determine the institution's tolerance for risk and, therefore, its expectations for endowment growth, and would approve an asset allocation policy.

Since endowment assets are invested for the long term, and since income from endowment is generally important, the board's decisions about the allocation of assets are a critical responsibility. It is an expression of the board's tolerance for risk, measured in the range of fluctuation in value, versus potential growth of assets.

Beyond rational asset allocation, there is a need for boards to respect the wishes of donors with respect to the use of their donated funds. In most states the written wishes of the donors must be followed. Many schools, however, at one time or another "borrow" against those permanently restricted funds. Sometimes, but not always, they pay interest to the endowment to make up for the reduced investment returns. From a legal point of view, that is problematic. From the point of view of a potential donor doing due diligence about the school's use and care of donated funds, sloppy treatment of endowment funds is a turn off.

The head of one institution, which had very large interfund balances resulting from "borrowing" money from restricted funds, stated that "we have indeed depleted undesignated reserves ... (and) restricted, designated, and undesignated reserves...." But as explanation he notes that "our fiduciary responsibility is not as simple as guarding assets in the bank. It is about using resources wisely and appropriately for the purposes for which they were given, which is education."

That is misleading. The responsibility of the board is to use the funds for the specific written uses the donor specified. Reorienting their use for a different, broader, purpose is not appropriate, and is probably not legal. Furthermore, I would argue that fiduciary responsibility for any ongoing organization is to make sure that it will be able to carry out its mission into the future. That means a solid and healthy balance sheet, which guards restricted funds to ensure that their income is available to support mission going forward, and unrestricted annual income sufficient for the various operating expenses necessary to support mission.

Borrowing long term funds for short-term goals is not generally a wise policy.

It is very difficult for a nonprofit in general, and schools in particular, to fail to support projects or programs that are seen as critical to mission. But resources are always limited and perceived needs are unlimited; the business of the organization is to bring those elements into balance.

Schools require faculties and facilities. Endowment, plant and faculty assets represent assets that need to be built and maintained. It is the responsibility of the board to make sure that those assets are properly tended so that the institution remains viable and effective.

Stewardship of Facilities

Facilities are as a much a part of the endowment of a school as invested funds, but generally do not get the same care and attention by trustees. For many schools the value of plant and equipment far exceeds the value of invested capital. The reasons that trustees fail in proper facilities management are at least three: insufficient financial resources, poor judgment, and inadequate capability.

When budgets are tight, facilities maintenance usually suffers. There is a false sense of permanence with buildings, a kind of Newtonian Law that states that buildings once built will stay as built, that systems can always be fixed, roofs repaired, pavement patched. That notion makes a kind of intuitive sense, and that is perhaps why maintenance is commonly delayed. It even has its own name, "deferred maintenance," which is the work that should have been done and ultimately will be done, albeit at a much higher cost. The money that should go to timely maintenance is spent on salaries or program and nobody sees that redirection in the short run.

The sense of permanence has some validity. School facilities far outlast their depreciation schedule. Of course buildings are actually aging, but from one day to the next there is no discernible difference. We get used to the condition of the facility as it slowly degrades.

There was a request for new blinds on a classroom casement window because the old ones were ripped and torn. The problem, however, was that the blinds would have to be installed several inches in from the window because the window was broken; the top was leaning into the classroom and could not be closed. A teacher who had been using that room for many years stated that it had been in that condition as long as she had been there, some 17 years! She was told it could not be fixed. In fact, there had been at some distant time a wasps nest built in part of the opening which, when removed, allowed the window to close easily. That was a great surprise to the teacher. Something that can be fixed, left long enough unfixed, becomes unfixable.

Facilities also deteriorate because of lack of discernment, which is the inability to see the deterioration of the facilities either physically or mentally. It also includes the failure to understand how facilities both support program and are perceived by parents and students to reflect program. Facilities are not kept up because there is a lack of interest in their maintenance from the top and little understanding of their financial and programmatic value. The lack of vision often causes a lack of capability, certainly a lack of interest, among those who are specifically responsible for building maintenance and improvement.

Facilities are, in major markets, also elements by which schools compete for the best students. Even in suburban schools where there may be less choice, parents who cannot easily evaluate the quality of teaching, can evaluate the quality of building maintenance, and may assume the one reflects the other.

The lack of upkeep capability is partially a result of both the finances of the school and the vision of those responsible for its stewardship. Lack of capability is not the responsibility of the maintenance crew, but rather of the administration and the board. It exists when nobody cares enough to fix it. It manifests itself in financial and in physical ways. Many schools contract out the most basic jobs, such as replacing panes of glass, minor painting, repairing knobs and locks. Many schools will do jobs themselves, but poorly.

A dormitory master's bedroom ceiling leaked. In fact, on three separate occasions the plaster roof itself fell in large pieces onto the master's bed. The ceiling was under a bathroom on the floor above and in each case the bathroom tile floor was examined, fittings tightened, caulked, re-embedded. Eventually the showers above were examined carefully. It was found that instead of a proper shower pan, the tiles were laid over a green plastic trash bag, which was leaking. In addition to the continuing devastation of the ceiling panels, the joists were at that point also beginning to rot. It was not because the ceiling fell three times that the problem was finally fixed; it was because a newly invigorated facilities manager started to work for a new business manager who began to ask the right questions. "Do it right the first time" was a new idea!

There are at least three kinds of maintenance to consider, not including "deferred" maintenance. Deferred maintenance may be made up of undone maintenance from any of the following categories.

Normal maintenance. This goes on daily. Normal maintenance includes mowing the grass, repairing faucets, painting classrooms, changing filters and the thousand details required to keep property working well and looking good (the two are inseparable). If done carefully, normal maintenance is like a healthy lifestyle: it doesn't guarantee that major maintenance will not be needed, but it does reduce the likelihood of unexpected and unplanned maintenance.

Capital maintenance is work that can be planned for and includes major work such as replacing a roof or re-surfacing parking lots or replacement of heating or air conditioning systems or, indeed, construction or major renovation of buildings.

Routine upgrading and reorganizing is work that should be routinely planned for as maintenance and seldom is; that is work to reconfigure space for new or changed curricular or non-curricular use.

The quality of maintenance of facilities that I am calling "stewardship" is more than about buildings and mechanical systems.

How the plant is cared for sends a very powerful, if sometimes subtle, message to the school's constituencies. Those who have prepared a house for sale will understand the message. If the home is tastefully but simply furnished, is clean and freshly painted, perhaps with flowers on the mantle and even a fresh baked loaf of bread on the kitchen table, the appeal is clear and immediate. If the house needs paint, dog toys are strewn on the floor or there are dirty dishes in the sink, potential buyers will be embarrassed and want to leave, not buy.

In a tired school with too few classrooms and labs, the administration decided that the program was too good and its faculty too strong to risk the perception that new parents might base on the buildings and grounds which had been poorly maintained and looked it. Pending implementation of a master facilities plan, the school began an annual planting day, involving parents, students, and staff in overhauling the landscaping to a more colorful and obviously cared for campus. An old and revered tree was perhaps unintentionally symbolic of the situation. It was heavily wired together, having lost most of its crown. After much hand wringing and impatient argument it was replaced by a handsome red maple. The beautiful new tree was not the symbol the old one had been: it was instead an inadvertent symbol of how things were now.

The medium is the message; broad involvement of constituencies and attention to detail and appearances is seen as caring about the institution. It is not always clear which comes first, the caring that gives rise to the stewardship or the manipulation of perception that gives rise to the opportunity for caring. Either way, facilities do send a message that is clear to most observers. Trustees, in their role as stewards of their institutions, need to pay attention to their large investment in buildings and land.

Chapter 7

Planning

Planning is critically important for any healthy organization. It is the process by which we try to manage our future. This chapter describes two very different approaches to planning, one external and the other internal. The first is called "strategic planning" and the second "Strategic Envisioning©."

Strategic Planning

Strategic planning sets goals to support the school's mission. These are strategic goals, broadly drawn, that take into account the external environment in which the school operates. Strategic planning requires an institution to do a thorough assessment of the environment in which it operates and a careful analysis of how it can best use its resources to create a sustainable competitive advantage. It is a process that focuses on efficient management of resources to obtain measurable goals—which may be different from its current set of goals.

Consideration must be given to the competitive market for students, the economy that may affect parents' ability to pay, demographic trends that affect the pool of applicants, the regulatory atmosphere within which the school has to negotiate to build or renovate facilities, and environmental trends that may affect its ability to expand or even remain at its location. Strategic planning is a process designed to develop and maintain a sustained competitive advantage within its environment. Strategic planning questions whether the environment can support the institution and may require the school to take action to change its mission or perhaps to move if it cannot.

Proper strategic planning, as defined here, is seldom done by schools for a variety of reasons. First, it is not very glamorous work, not the kind that will excite the constituencies the school wants to energize (usually in preparation for a capital funds drive). Second, it is hard work that takes diligent, detailed effort with exacting analysis of trends, in other words acquisition, organization and objective review of lots of numbers. Third, after environmental and demographic analysis is completed, strategic planning requires objective review of how the school's curriculum, faculty, facilities and financial underpinnings relate to the analysis of the environment within which it operates. It further requires adjustment of those essential school elements to ensure that they will fit what the analysis indicates will be their environment in the future. Fourth, boards and administrators believe themselves responsible for the present success of the school and that it will, therefore, continue. Alternatively, if the school is in dire straits the board is usually fully engaged in saving it despite the fact that careful strategic planning might result in an orderly closing of the school or a merger or a refocusing, any of which might better position the school for a successful future than a futile effort to save it as it is.

Moreover, strategic planning carries with it an assumption that there is a market for school services and it is the market that determines what the school should offer rather than the other way around. That notion is anathema to some boards and many heads of schools.

Most boards undertake what they call "strategic planning" episodically, often in conjunction with decennial accreditation activities. Energy is expended by large task forces of parents, students, teachers and others whose job it is to look at the strengths and weaknesses of the school and figure out how to build on strengths and shore up weaknesses. Plans based on those studies are supposed to guide the activities of the school until the next planning period.

A Vision from Values: Strategic Envisioning

"Strategic Envisioning," on the other hand, focuses on capturing the energy of people working toward a commonly held vision of what an organization can accomplish and how it carries out its work. Strategic planning is external to the school's work while strategic envisioning is internal.

Strategic Envisioning is a new planning process that fits the way nonprofits actually work. It recognizes imperfect information, limited resources and the resistance to change of both structures and cultures. That resistance is, paradoxically, a strength for a nonprofit because in a healthy organization it derives from a commitment to a set of core values that are the heart of the organization. Strategic Envisioning builds on that strength and recognizes weaknesses as opportunities for better alignment with those core values.

Strategic Envisioning asks just three fundamental questions:

- How do we want to be perceived (what is our vision?) and
- What are we doing that contributes to that vision, and
- What would we like to do better?

The goal of Strategic Envisioning is to use the power of a widely held and clearly articulated vision to transform the organization by aligning as closely as possible its structure and operation with that vision. The process of Strategic Envisioning helps to build in the school's community the capacity to embrace its intent and its consequences.

The six steps of Strategic Envisioning are as follows:

1. Determine the core values that constituents believe uniquely describe the essence of the organization. Core values may include a specific pedagogy (Montessori Schools, the "Orton-Gillingham" method of working with dyslexic children) or approach (single sex schools) or a belief (community service) or any other characteristic or attitude that is central to what attracts people to the school.

2. Create a coherent institutional vision statement that subsumes those values.

3. Test that vision against a consensus understanding of how the school really works. (Does it make sense?).

4. Identify elements of the structure and operation of the organization that support the vision and, as importantly, those that do not. It is important to step back and look at what has been described with clear eyes. A group of people may believe fervently in a set of values that have no currency in the world as it exists. (There will probably be no more Shaker communities, regardless of those who believe in the ethic demonstrated by the work of those communities.)

5. Develop goals and objectives to capitalize on positive elements and to address weaknesses. Many boarding schools have survived by providing specialized services quite different from those on which they were founded. If your organization depends upon attracting a specific clientele, it is reasonable to determine if there is a demonstrated supply of such people.

6. Recognize that this is an iterative process; that is, each of these steps should explicitly be reviewed annually at a board meeting. The community as a whole, with the leadership of the board, should repeat the entire process every five years.

The repetition noted above is necessary because this is a self-correcting process. The articulation of values will change as members of the various constituencies change, as the economic, social and demographic environment changes and as the organization as a whole learns how this all really works. The resulting changes will tend to keep the organization relevant to the society in which it operates.

It is important that this be an open process including both internal and external constituencies. The organization will change, subtly and slowly, but inexorably. Change involves individual compromises in support of community vision. It is therefore critical that the vision be widely supported and that processes in support of the vision are widely understood.

Unlike the change resulting from strategic planning, that which comes from Strategic Envisioning is internally driven, deriving its success from the common bond of people with a shared vision. It is, for that reason, very powerful and far less frightening than "strategic planning" for those involved.

I stated at the beginning of this chapter that planning has as its goal the development and maintenance of a sustainable competitive advantage. Whether they want to talk about it or not, schools are in competition: private versus private; girls versus boys; boarding versus day, institutional versus home schooling.

Schools find it hard to evaluate their students' needs in the light of changing values, information and expectations, and then to redesign curriculum to reflect how students know, think and live. Schools do not want to think of themselves as an "education delivery system" which produces that body of skills and knowledge that will get students into the "best" colleges and jobs. But why else do most parents ultimately send their children at great cost to these schools? Schools that don't get it will fall by the wayside or end up with a student population they do not want and cannot serve.

Most private schools are tuition driven. If they fail to attract students and necessary funds to support programming, whether through ineffective marketing, a lackluster curriculum or an inadequate pool of students the school will fail outright or change. It might become a school very different from what people thought they knew about it — probably not a turn for the better.

With 13 percent of United States students educated in non-public schools, and a large number of schools competing for students, it is not unreasonable to ask how independent schools expect to attract and retain faculty, staff and students, and what the demands of successful and attractive schools are on facilities, curriculum, operating cash, capital needs, etc.

A plan to develop and maintain a sustainable competitive advantage requires answers to four simple questions, using four different analyses:

- How big will the target population be? (demographics)
- Can that population pay the bills? (economics)
- Who is our competition now, and who will it be in the future? (competitive analysis and projections)
- What skills and abilities will students need and what programs do we have to develop and supply their needs? (programmatic)

The defining question for the board is: if it had the answers to those questions, what would it do with them? That is precisely the point of planning: to evaluate the environment and values to generate answers to the global, and harder, questions.

- What should a school do if its target population is in decline?
- How should the board react to an analysis that projects a falling market or a high unemployment rate?
- Should the school administration change its curriculum from what is currently successful to a new structure based on projections of competitive curricular trends?
- How should the school define itself and its product in the splintering educational environment?

Strategic Planning is a difficult process and often leads to difficult questions. It looks outside to the environment and may require difficult changes to the institution driven by that external environment. It may threaten the school because it is external to its culture.

But most nonprofits, because of their complex communities of constituents, cannot easily restructure themselves to exploit what such planning might conclude. Similarly, an Episcopal church is unlikely to do a market analysis and decide that it would grow faster if it embraced the Unitarian/Universalist persuasion. Strategic Envisioning will not force such issues but will, as stated, produce incremental change.

Chapter 8

Mission Statements

It is the particular role of trustees to satisfy themselves that the implementation of the mission of the institution supports its vision. In order to carry out this responsibility, the board has to assure itself that the mission is correctly articulated for the environment in which the institution expects to function in the foreseeable future. "A mission has to be operational, otherwise its just good intentions."[1]

Schools are generally founded by a person with a vision of how a group of students might be successfully educated. Mission, in a sense, materializes the vision, breaks it down into actionable steps. This can happen without a mission statement when ways of teaching, relating and learning attain the status of tradition, "The Academy Way." This will remain in place so long as things don't change too much or too quickly and so long as trustees understand and support the founding vision and make sure it is translated into a structure and process that is relevant to the school's environment.

Nevertheless, most schools feel a need to generate a mission statement, sometimes and perhaps more accurately called a statement of objectives and purposes. This may happen when there is a change of head of school, or as part of the decennial accreditation process, or when a school grows or changes significantly. It is an attempt to describe what the school does and how it does it, hopefully in a way that differentiates it from its competition and is attractive to potential students. Mission statements rarely work well as educational guidelines, however, because they generally lack clear and measurable goals.

For most of us, a mission is a journey to a specific place with clear goals and objectives undertaken with a given set of procedures by people trained to do the job. That does not describe the mission statements generally written by schools. They usually are developed as a result of a "strategic planning" exercise, the purpose of which in business is to develop a sustainable competitive advantage. As noted earlier, strategic planning is something schools, and most nonprofits, cannot and do not successfully complete.

Strategic planning and a more useful alternative "strategic envisioning" are discussed in another chapter. For the purpose of this discussion of mission, strategic planning should be thought of as both the source and test of the validity of a school's vision/mission. This can be illustrated with slightly edited examples from real schools. The visions behind the mission statements are deduced because none are expressed.

School "A" Mission Statement

School A is an independent, coeducational, K-12, college preparatory day school of 300 students. Set amid resources of a large metropolitan city, the site itself is historic.

As a small school, we continually seek different cultures, races, interests and perspectives. Our community supports and celebrates a number of dichotomies: We emphasize both faculty individuality and widespread collaboration. We value both traditional academic rigor and innovative methods of teaching, such as cross-disciplinary approaches, independent study, and the incorporation of technology into many facets of our curriculum. We encourage both a deep sense of each person's accountability to the school community and a relaxed atmosphere unencumbered by elaborate rules. In all areas – academic, artistic, and athletic – we applaud high achievement while promoting a philosophy of nurtured risk taking.

Fundamental to the success of these policies is our determination to give students freedom in manageable increments as they pass from lower to middle to upper school. Leading them through their journeys is a committed, highly responsive faculty of life-long learners who are able to teach small classes because of the priority the School places on a remarkably low ratio of students to teachers. The interactions within a strong and diverse set of students and teachers stand at the center of our school's education.

The School joins with the parents to galvanize the intellectual and creative capabilities of each student, to equip each to excel in future academic endeavors, and to instill in each the self-reliance and moral awareness to identify and work through life's challenges. Our mission is to prepare our students to be healthy, responsible, and informed adults who will play an active role in improving the world they will inherit.

This statement was a community effort, revised and rewritten over a significant period of time. While there was considerable editing for style and expression, there was a very high level of agreement over content. All parties were proud of the process and the outcome. As a statement of mission, however, like most school mission statements, it misses the mark. It does not have the hard clarity of "fuel the space ship, send men to the moon, pick up rock samples and return safely to Earth."

What is the difference? Except for its self-description as "college preparatory," it is not until the end that the statement makes any declarative attempt to describe outcomes: "equip each (student) to excel in future academic endeavors" and "instill self-reliance and moral awareness." The final sentence which actually begins "Our mission is" wanders through desired characteristics of graduates before getting to something with more of a mission feel to it: to prepare students "who will play an active role in improving the world they will inherit." The implication of the statement is that there are prescriptive ways to accomplish that "preparation" and that "improving the world" is a useful activity.

What is missing is any standard by which either the preparation or the improvement can be measured. It is, therefore, a statement of values, not of vision. What it captures is an idea of how a good school can operate. As such, it may well represent the views of the school community and be a valuable piece of work. However, it does not provide any sense of how embedded those values are in the curriculum nor how to measure the success of their implementation. There is no "therefore." The question of the value or success in the marketplace of a school that has the characteristics stated in the mission statement is not addressed. It is not a document from which a board of trustees can build an agenda or evaluate how well it is upholding its trust. It does not appear to result from or support the goals of a strategic plan.

The vision of this first school could have been stated as follows: "A child-centered, active learning school where teachers are guides and mentors and children are given the opportunity to develop their creative, critical and moral faculties in an atmosphere of mutual respect and support." A lot of educators would find that hard to disparage.

While mission statement A suggests a general purpose, the next sample statement, also from a real school with similar values, is somewhat different.

School "B" Mission Statement

School B is committed to providing outstanding preschool, elementary, and college preparatory education to qualified students. The School distinguishes itself through the excellence of its instruction and by providing a challenging but supportive environment for its students. Its objective is to maximize the potential of each child.

The School attracts a culturally diverse group of students possessing a variety of talents and skills, each student being expected to contribute to and benefit from the stimulating environment. An important aspect of that environment is the students' appreciation of and respect for each other. The School seeks to provide sufficient financial assistance to insure that all highly qualified children will have access to the School.

The School attracts the best available faculty by providing outstanding facilities, caring and responsible students, and a supportive environment. The School offers competitive compensation, opportunities for career-long professional development, and participation in decision making.

As a college preparatory school, the School prepares young men and women for success in the colleges and universities which fit their needs, interests, and capabilities. The School's goal is for colleges and universities to recognize it as a superior school addressing its students' ethical, social, cultural, and physical development as well as their academic preparation.

The School is an exemplary citizen, playing an active role in the community by providing an outstanding educational experience for the community's children and by offering its resources and facilities for wider community use. Its staff and student body participate actively in community affairs.

The School recognizes its obligation to its alumni, friends, and other benefactors, not only to carry out its mission of academic excellence but also to conduct its affairs responsibly.

The School graduates intellectually curious and academically competent young men and women who are well prepared for college, who care about each other and the world around them, who have an understanding of major global issues, and who are stimulated to be life-long learners.

This is not a bad mission statement. The school is committed to providing "an outstanding ... college preparatory education to qualified students." That can be measured (and I think is intended to be measured) by the school's college acceptance list. But even that paragraph ends with the wish to "maximize the potential of each child," whatever that means.

The next two paragraphs are statements of value, extolling "appreciation of and respect for each other." It wants to attract the "best available faculty" by providing to them "outstanding facilities, caring and responsible students, and a supportive environment...." It is interesting but not further developed (and also not measurable) that the school wants faculty to have the "opportunity" of "participation in decision making." In any case the third paragraph describes how the school wants to deal with faculty without any clear tie to how that will provide a better education to its students. Clearly it values "respect," "caring," and responsibility.

The fourth paragraph moves back to the promise of the first, emphasizing the college preparatory role of preparing its students for "success in the colleges and universities which fit their needs, interests, and capabilities." It is not clear, however, how it will address its "students' ethical, social, cultural and physical development," though it implies that those are valued aspects of a student's character that somehow should be considered.

Responsibility is important to School B, as its penultimate paragraph extols its obligation to "conduct its affairs responsibly." Its concluding paragraph ends with its desire (goal?) to graduate "intellectually curious" young men and women who "have an understanding of major global issues, and who are stimulated to be life-long learners." It is not clear how stimulation "to be life-long learners" can or will be measured.

The Useful Mission Statement

It is possible to write a useful mission statement for a school. The process begins with a board that understands the population being served and the factors that contribute to fulfilling the needs and expectations of that population. A successful mission statement cannot be written without or separately from solid strategic planning. The successful mission statement must also be tied to objective goals. The chapter on "Planning" enlarges this element of discussion. With the underpinning of successful planning, a real mission statement can be written – and actually used. Such a statement would include answers to the following questions:

- What population does this school serve?
- What are the outcomes that the population desires and towards which the school works?
- What distinguishes this school's methods for serving that population?

A bare-bones mission statement that answers those questions might be:

> XYZ Preparatory School seeks to serve day students within a half-hour radius of the school, in grades 9-12, who have the demonstrated academic skills and emotional stability to work

collaboratively in a rigorous academic program to prepare for admittance to a broad range of colleges and universities appropriate for their interests and capabilities. The School values creativity and recognizes that academics alone are not sufficient for adolescent boys and girls; active exposure to and participation in art, athletics, drama and music are therefore a requirement of the School. We believe in service and expect that all students will donate their time to support the School and the community we serve. We emphasize moral values in every aspect of our program and =expect that our families will support the education of students who are capable of independent thinking and of making appropriate choices for future education.

The population served is within a specific geographical area, has reasonable academic skills measured by college admission and does not have special emotional or learning issues. This is a college preparatory school, but emphatically does not prepare for competitive colleges and universities. The statement emphasizes "appropriate choices" for future education to underscore its commitment to serve students whose values are probably not Ivy League in nature. Co-curricular programs are deliberately stated to be part of the program, along with an interest in moral values and independent thinking.

Any mission statement should provide objectives for board evaluation by enrollment, faculty turnover, annual giving, operating trends and close study of where students go after graduation, how well they believe they are prepared for the choices they make and how well those choices work for them. The mission statement is clearly tied to the needs and expectations of the community from which the school draws students, and the school will work continually to ensure that what it does is attuned to what that community expects. In short, an effective mission statement represents not the school's point of view, but rather the point of view of the population it seeks to serve.

"Assessment and Mission Review" directly addresses measurement of mission. If there is one theme common to this entire volume, it is that education must be accountable and be organized for accountability. This is not accountability to some outside, arbitrary, entity but accountability to the constituencies that support it. The school is accountable for doing what it says it intends to do, and is accountable for clearly identifying and attracting those students for whom what it intends to do is appropriate and appealing. The mission statement (along with it supporting goals and objectives) should be the standard for accountability and provide the means by which to measure success. The responsibility for a clear mission statement and for operation of the school in a way that is consistent with that mission statement rests with the board of trustees.

[1] Druker, Peter. *Managing the Non-Profit Organization.* New York: Harper Business, 1992, p. 4.

Chapter 9

Assessment and Mission Review

Independent schools are generally free to design their own curricular and co-curricular programs, but they are usually subject to the 10-year accreditation cycle by which they study their own educational process and assess its strengths and weaknesses. This self-study is then reviewed by a group of peers under the umbrella of a regional accrediting organization that evaluates how well the school understands itself. The "visiting committee" then makes recommendations and issues commendations based on its assessment of how well the school supports its goals. This is a rigorous process, requiring each school to evaluate all areas of school life and to assess how well its policies and procedures support its mission. The report of the visiting team is received and the letter of accreditation framed and hung on the wall. Most schools heave a sigh of relief and go back to the daily work of education.

The fact is that depending on the evaluative instrument used by the accrediting organization, this decennial program is not nearly enough of a review of how well the school is fulfilling its mission and does not consider how relevant its mission is.

It would be instructive to be able to take a snapshot of an independent school at, say, 20- year intervals in which one could show how math is taught, what sports are offered and to whom, how discipline is managed and for what kinds of infractions, the background of students and faculty and the various other aspects that define the school experience. If those snapshots were on transparencies and stacked together, how consistent would the picture be over the life of the school?

Most schools do change, though at different rates because the expectations of their families and their faculties and staff change. Change in a well-managed, self-aware school will be a controlled change, resulting from a consistent effort by the board to evaluate the response to its mission statement and supporting goals and objectives. The board must make sure that it is still the right mission, given the environment in which the school operates.

Accreditation reviews are useful, but for most schools they are essentially formal exercises, required but not integral to the daily business of education. They can be useful as an external validation of an ongoing process of assessment and mission review. But properly done, that review is continuous, not episodic. Most thoughtful trustees and administrators understand the usual cycle:

- assess performance against mission,
- plan to build on strengths, address weaknesses,
- implement needed or desired changes,
- review effectiveness of implementation,
- and start again.

That usual cycle does not include mission review. Do we have the right mission for our population, for our economy, for our capability? Implicit in these chapters is the need to be sure that the institution's mission is clear and clearly communicated – and that it is relevant to its constituents. There is no point in assessing performance against a mission that no longer has an interested constituency. There is no point in being the best girls' boarding school in Connecticut if girls want to go to coed schools.

As essentially (and appropriately) conservative institutions, schools should not easily change properly researched and clearly articulated missions. Schools are conservators of knowledge, values and visions. Trustees should take their trust seriously. But the past recedes and the future becomes the present with new challenges and new opportunities along with new constituencies. Students know more and different things than their parents (and often their teachers). There are times when, because of external forces or the opportunities of new technology, change may be revolutionary. Schools that do not have a mechanism in place to assess the possible effects of change on their mission may find themselves out of business.

School & Mission Success Indicators

Assessment and mission review requires that school boards establish objective standards by which they can measure how well their mission fits the environment in which they operate. Success indicators can be grouped by students, faculty and staff, financial, facilities, and governance. In virtually every case, the trend is as important as the present reality.

Student Indicators
 a. Diversity
 b. Enrollment (inquiries, applications, acceptances and yield for targeted students)
 c. Attrition (voluntary vs. involuntary)
 d. College placement (percent accepted at first choice colleges & universities and percent attriting after matriculation from those first choice schools)

As an institution that depends on tuition income for its financial security, the engine is enrollment. Does the school attract the kinds of students for which it is organized? Schools that attract students who are not appropriate or whom the school is not able successfully to serve suffer severe consequences. And once attracted to the school, do the students stay? Attrition, like teacher turnover, has various causes, and a certain level is understandable and probably necessary. But above that level, it indicates either dissatisfaction or inappropriate placement. Students and their families vote with their feet, as well as their annual fund contributions. Enrollment trends are critical measures of the health of the institution.

Similarly, college placement measures the success of the school both in terms of the quality of education and in terms of the ability of the school to work with students and their families to agree on what constitutes an appropriate placement. Not everybody can or should go to Harvard. Good schools work with students and families to encourage and support their interest in colleges and universities that fit the student's skill, interest and personality. The test of the quality of that work is whether the student stays at the college to which he or she was accepted. If it was the correct choice, there will generally be a low number of transfers and dropouts.

Faculty and Staff Indicators
    a. Diversity
    b. Distribution by teaching experience
    c. Percentage with advanced degrees
    d. Quality of their own education
    e. Turnover (rates and reasons)

Recognizing that schools live off tuition, it is the faculty that defines the institution and ultimately delivers or does not deliver the program that attracts and retains the students. Turnover measures the satisfaction of individual faculty members with the institution and also measures, indirectly, the quality of the spread of faculty across age and experience. A very young faculty will have higher turnover than a faculty with a mix of age and experience. A good school will want some young faculty and the turnover that goes with that young faculty, but it will also want a core of committed and experienced teachers who provide stability and continuity to the program. A school that supports that kind of faculty will be a better school than one with a lot of turnover, both because of the expense and disruption of constant staff searches and replacements and because students and parents are put off by constant changes of personnel.

Financial Indicators
    a. Budget vs. actual
    b. Cash flow
    c. Net asset growth
    d. Annual giving
    e. Accounts receivable
    f. Capital campaign results
    g. Operating funds
    h. Professional development funds availability
    i. Ratio trends (debt coverage, department expense percentage, endowment per student, return on investment)
    j. Resource allocation (analysis of extra-classroom support of students)

As with attrition, the annual appeal, which targets parents and graduates, provides an annual referendum for how the school is perceived to be doing. If parents are comfortable and committed, they show that through their gifts. If they are uncomfortable, they withhold their gifts.

Donors, especially major donors, may well look at the growth of the school's net assets and the trends of the operating fund. Because a school is nonprofit (501(c)(3)), that does not mean that it can afford for long to spend more than it takes in. School budgets should be managed to provide the change in net assets (surplus/deficit) that the school needs, to avoid having to dip into its own capital. There should be a clean audited statement that clearly illustrates the strength of the school's management of its fiscal and facility assets.

Facilities Indicators
    a. Maintenance per square foot
    b. Capital budget vs. identified capital needs
    c. General purpose and specialty classrooms utilization percentage
    d. How do the facilities look?

The facilities, the "hard" assets, are important not so much because they are the necessary location of the education process, but for what they demonstrate about the school's general management of its assets. Physical plant notoriously does not get sufficient attention, especially in times when budgets are tight. They do not deteriorate so quickly that a short period of abandonment will irretrievably ruin them. But deferred maintenance is more expensive maintenance, and a well-run institution will avoid it at all costs.

If maintenance costs are well above or below benchmarks, there is a problem. If there is no capital budget, or if it is unfunded, there is a problem. As a general rule, classroom utilization of 85 percent or higher means that classrooms are over-utilized; when that happens, schedules are distorted and programs suffer. Overcrowding indicates that some sections are not being offered, or that they are not convenient for students who want to take them. If that is the situation, how did it happen and what is the school doing about it? If classroom utilization is too high because enrollment has increased and the school has a plan to correct it, then all is well. If there is no plan, that is a problem to be considered.

Governance
    a. Frequency of mission revision
    b. Board turnover (rate and reasons)
    c. Board meeting attendance
    d. Trustee committee involvement

Assessment and Mission Review is not difficult if the board requires it and is willing to follow through. The indicators do not directly measure the "quality" of education, of course, but they indirectly measure the factors that are necessary for a high-quality education. It is very likely that the school is a good school if these indicators are positive. It is conversely likely that the school is in trouble if these indicators are negative.

These are not complicated measures but they must be made against clear objectives and standards, and must be undertaken to ensure continued relevance and quality. The further and more important point is that measurement will not take place without a committed board able to direct and support such an effort and willing to accept and implement its conclusions.

Chapter 10

Negotiating Change

Change is the only constant, yet our governing boards act as though nothing changes. The fact is that everything changes in our society, in our culture, in our economy. It is an industry joke that a 19th century teacher could walk into many of our classrooms and, except for some substitution of tools (computer for slate) much the same techniques that worked in 1809 would work in 2009; the class and the process would look much the same. That might superficially be true. But we now have a global economy and multinational companies and do much business and almost all administrative functions with and through technology. The teacher of two centuries ago might recognize the classroom and even the subjects, but the business of education is (or should be) squarely aimed at helping students learn how to learn and learn how to work collaboratively. Not all schools, colleges and universities have gotten there, but they will focus on what their students need to know or will disappear.

The school must change because the students' needs change; their technological sophistication has changed totally and the skills they need to succeed in life have changed. The ability of an individual to keep up with the evolution (revolution?) of information technology is now a critical life skill that cannot be taught with the old tools. Students must experience how to use these tools, which has layered a whole new curriculum on what is still in many schools the 19th century curriculum their parents were still learning in the mid 20th century.

We actually don't have much control over accepting change, but we perhaps reflexively try to avoid bringing change on ourselves. We buy a house in the nice neighborhood and do not want zoning to change in a way that threatens our view or peace. I have stated in other chapters that schools must update their missions to keep up with the needs of their market, which certainly does change. They must be prepared to compete with other schools or other types of schooling if they want to remain relevant and effective (and solvent). It is uniquely the role of the board to look into the future and make the corrections to course that will guide the institution safely into the future.

Accepting change is easier than making the decision to change. That decision process is difficult for a variety of reasons. Knowing what decisions to make requires a commitment to engage with issues and with environmental variables. Most difficult of all, however, is a willingness to take a risk with community relationships. After all, decisions ultimately must be embraced by the community which has made a commitment to an enterprise that you are suggesting may no longer be worthy of that commitment.

All too often administrators or board members want the support of parents or of community boards and commissions for some project that will effect change. If the petitioned party does not agree with or immediately recognize the validity of the project, the school administration, convinced that the request is absolutely legitimate and, indeed, self-evidently true becomes frustrated. Its arguments may include some of the following:

- Enrollment is up so more classrooms are needed.
- The new facility will enhance our ability to attract students.
- The construction of new dorms (or library) will provide jobs for local contractors.

While the message is (for example) that the school wants to build a new facility, neighbors or town boards or city commissions hear: "their enrollment is up so they can afford new competitive facilities which will attract more students and further increase enrollment." They fear the loss of what they know and are used to.

Town boards also hear that there will be more traffic from increased enrollment, more out of town families clogging their neighborhood, more kids hanging around or driving around and that the school will have a larger impact in the community. The community may not want the school to expand beyond its current size and has not been given any information from which to conclude that there is any need for further growth. In this scenario, the school is unlikely to get the permits it wants.

What the town or city boards or commissions need is data that will lead their members to agree with the school that growth is good for the school and good for the community. That means that the school needs to develop good (objective) data, be willing to share that data and recognize the legitimate interests of the community as well as its own interests. That willingness to treat the recipient of communication as a partner is essential to communication success.

As I have framed this, it sounds like communication is an element of negotiation. I believe that is precisely the case.

When a school goes to the local planning board, it is already in a negotiation situation and might as well recognize that reality. Negotiation is, at its basic level, back-and-forth communication designed to reach an agreement when you and the other side have some interests that may be shared and others that are probably opposite.

Typically, before you get to the planning board or the community group, people in the community have an idea that something is afoot. They have seen survey stakes in a field; faculty have talked with friends in town or in their apartment building. On the town or city side, people who have noticed activity or heard about the school's plans are wondering why there has been no communication. "Are they going to bully their way through this as they always do?" There may be letters to the editor decrying the (potential) expansion or letters from the school to parents and other constituents announcing a fundraising campaign to support the wonderful new facility. With these letters, discussions in front of community groups (and at cocktail parties), along with other formal and informal communications to constituents, there is clearly communication and negotiation going on—but the parties are not talking directly to each other.

A Relationship: Listening and Sharing

While I was overseeing major construction at a school in a residential neighborhood of a city, another school up the road was similarly engaged. That school's neighbors were in full cry. They were angry. They felt that the school was running roughshod over their legitimate interests and used every method they could think of to stop the project.

Our project, on the other hand, had none of that rancor. That was not the result of a project that was unnoticeable, but rather because we had started to talk with the neighbors two years before we were to start the project. We invited them to come in and talk with us and the architect over tea or sherry. We visited neighbors who could not make our meetings. We showed them what we were doing and why we were doing it. We also agreed to an enrollment level (above our then current enrollment) that would be appropriate for the kind of school we wanted to be. We listened to the neighbors and made some changes in design and placement of facilities.

We built a relationship through honest and early discussions that allowed us to talk about construction problems that were, for some, very annoying instead of fighting about them. We stayed available and visible during the construction so that if things did not go well the administration was clearly present and working to solve problems.

It is a critical preparatory step in communications to develop a relationship before trying to develop an agreement. The goal of any purposeful communication or negotiation is an agreement that satisfies our interests and can hold up over time. If the relationship is antagonistic it will be very hard for the parties to really hear what each is saying. Every communication will appear to have an ulterior motive unrelated to the actual subject. It will be the perceived motive that will get the attention of the parties, not the proposed subject.

In order to reach a desired agreement, the board and the school should
1. be very clear about the school's long-term interests,
2. be very clear about the long-term interests of the other party to the negotiation,
3. understand what the school's options are,
4. understand the options of the other party,
5. be clear about how well those options relate to our and their interests.

The board and administration should prepare a case for an outcome or range of outcomes that are best for the school. That preparation should also provide strategies to help successfully "sell" the solution to their constituencies (faculty, parents, students, graduates, municipal and state agencies).

The board and administration should also anticipate implementation problems that might well arise, should the proposals be accepted, and figure out ahead of time how to overcome those problems. Below is an example of a preliminary list of interests and goals for a school and its host community.

School	Community
Competitive facilities	Retain the "character" of the town
Dormitories	Limit building density
Classrooms and laboratories	Preserve resources
First class athletic facilities	Water
Recruitment of able students	Open land
Increased endowment from capital campaigns and planned giving	Attractive vistas
Competitive faculty salaries	Retain social values of the town
Competitive tuition and financial aid	Control traffic density and movement
Affordable faculty housing	Support a viable business climate
Recognition as an excellent school	Preserve the tax base

There are no doubt many other goals for any given school and its community. There are probably some shared interests (is faculty easier to recruit because of the location and character of the town?). Does the school location allow an extensive, high quality program that is specific to the characteristics of that location and would be hard to match elsewhere? For example, there could be a high quality competitive skiing program for a school with easy access to a ski area. There could be crew or sailing for a school on a river or lake. Better yet, these programs could be opened up to students in town schools as a way to enrich their programs by giving them access to options they otherwise would not have.

Make no mistake: this approach to communication and negotiation is very deliberate and requires considerable discipline. It requires clear priorities and goals both for the immediate needs of the school and for development of a longer term relationship that can support the interests of both the school and the community over time.

The communication/negotiation team that will deal with the interests and goals of the parties should be a consultative group, not a decision-making group, the members of which will make recommendations to their respective decisions makers. The immediate first challenge is to build relationships from which serious discussion can proceed, and the presence of decision makers at those initial discussions will raise the stakes too high for the kind of relationship building discussion that has to take place in the beginning of this process.

It is generally best if the head of school and president of the board have an up-front and public role, but the bulk of serious conversation should be held between people who are not the senior decision makers for their entities but rather people who can be free to consider various options because they cannot commit or decide among those options,

While there needs to be a deliberate process of communication, it is not a mechanical process. It is hard work and takes a lot of time to think about how an individual or group hears what you are saying. Once you do spend the time and effort to understand how what people hear varies from what you think you are saying, you are engaged in real communication.

The head of school left suddenly in late fall and rumors increased by the hour about the reasons for the departure. Some thought the head had been fired after being unfairly judged, other had an opposite view. A small crisis committee was convened and a process of communicating to the various school constituencies began. The group had two goals: make sure that it had the facts and demonstrate that the leadership in place was managing the crisis effectively, especially with respect to the safety and education of the children.

The communications program the group developed was very hard work, took a lot of time and required the crisis group to really think hard about what people wanted and needed to hear. It was successful. Students and faculty did not leave as a result of this shock to the community. Once people felt they were being told the truth—that the school felt the various constituencies deserved the truth—the fear of the unknown mostly went away and the school went about the business of educating children. In fact, the crisis communiqués stopped only after a number of people said "enough, we have all the information we need."

Once you are in real communication you will find that while there still may be disagreements that cannot be resolved, you will be dealing with issues rather than with unintended consequences of a communication process that engages emotions rather than minds. It is amazing what can be done when people are really talking with each other about things they care about. In the intellectual life that schools are in business to support and enrich, working hard to communicate ideas effectively is well worth the effort. It may indeed be the whole game.

Chapter 11

Technology – A Speculation for Thoughtful Trustees

The promise of small and relatively cheap computers coupled with easy access to the Internet has the potential to revolutionize education. It has already dramatically increased the cost of providing education in schools by three to five percent. But the operative word is still "potential." The integration of technology, specifically computers, specialized application software and Internet access into curricula is spotty at best despite the proliferation of computers in schools. Even in schools that have embraced programs that provide or require computers for all or most students, presumably at the forefront of technological sophistication, the range of utilization of these tools varies dramatically.

Technology is a good example of the issues faced by schools seeking that all-important competitive edge. It is relatively clumsy to integrate into curriculum but even more importantly, it is difficult to assess its contribution to learning. As budgets are built, planning groups are convened and curriculum is reviewed, we should ask how the administration can make the case for new expenditures of hundreds of thousands of dollars from an already tight budget, on what grounds the board can approve those expenditures, and how will the educational value of those expenditures be evaluated?

Personal Computers (PCs) have been around for a very short time. For most individuals, the introduction of the IBM PC in 1983 with Microsoft's Disk Operating System (DOS) marked the legitimate beginning of the personal computer revolution. While there were small, relatively cheap computers well before that, IBM legitimized the category. VisiCalc, the spreadsheet that is the direct ancestor of today's powerful modeling tools, was introduced for the Apple II in 1979 and made that computer something more than an idle toy. It was the first "killer application" that enabled users to do serious work on a personal computer.

"Technology" as a word predates its current association with computers and networks by well over 2,000 years. The Greeks said it first, of course, and meant the "systematic treatment of an art."[1] It means to us, as it has since the 18th century, "the practical application of knowledge"[2] especially in a particular area. What is happening today is only the latest instance in the long history of increasing the speed and breadth of the transfer of information. The innovations of the telegraph (Samuel F.B. Morse, 1840); the telephone (Alexander Graham Bell, 1876); radio (Guglielmo Marconi, 1897); and television (Philo T. Farnsworth, 1930) allowed the transmission speed of information to increase at the same time as the amount of information being transmitted increased.

Notice the progression: coded point-to-point information (the telegraph); audio point-to-point information (telephone); broadcast one-way audio information (radio); broadcast one-way audio and video (television). The Internet promises to put it all together. With digital technology, the Internet will combine broadcast and multiple (interactive) point-to-point transmission of audio and video (moving and still).

All "information," taken broadly, will be available instantly; and an unimaginable number of people will be in communication with each other in varying combinations. Much of that potential is actually available now in sophisticated or rudimentary form. It is not too hard to see the capability of this connectivity. Or its inevitability.

What is hard to understand is how to harness its potential to improve society. Education is a conservative business, and is getting further behind the curve as transfer of information becomes easier and cheaper and the tools become more nearly ubiquitous. Before it can transform society, of course, technology must transform education. It has a long way to go.

At heart schools fail to fully integrate technology into their curricula because it is hard to do. Technology at its most useful is not simply a tool; it is a process. It does not, like an overhead projector, simply allow the entire class to see the same thing at the same time. It enables each student to see, manipulate and interact with his or her own version of the object being projected. It represents an approach to education that is totally opposite to most modern education. The teacher has the potential to guide or coach each student individually, with each at a different place in the learning process. It has the potential to split classes and courses into a number of pieces equal to the number of students.

Even in progressive schools where, as the mission statement usually reads, "each student's inherent ability and motivation to learn" are recognized, and the emphasis is on "critical and independent thinking," this nevertheless often happens in a "structured academic environment." If the heart of education is learning, and clearly students learn at different rates in different ways, if technology has the power to support and guide those differences, who benefits from the "structured academic environment"?

In fact, technology has the potential to reverse the paradigm. The structured environment could be provided by technology in the transforming power given to the individual to learn interactively in the environment he or she chooses, whether in a school, a museum, in a park or at home. That environment will increasingly not be provided by the academic institution and need not be. Schools may, in a sense, become physical resource centers, while the intellectual resource centers will be on the Internet. Academies may provide, as needed by the learners, laboratory space, gymnasiums, spaces where certain art and music activities can be organized, and guidance and counseling centers, where "teachers" help students to assess their programs of learning and work with students whose learning styles are impeding their learning (though much of that will be resolved with more intelligent software that will respond proactively to differences in learning capabilities).

For any of this to happen productively, the unthinkable also has to happen; schools must reinvent themselves in a revolutionary, not evolutionary, way. Planning, as is noted elsewhere in this book, is seldom done, and rarely well. Besides being hard work, it also requires an examination of the environment in which the school operates and an evaluation of whether the school's services are needed or wanted by that environment, which can be unsettling to a board or administration. Serious planning has the potential, as in the case of technology, to result in an acknowledgement that the environment no longer requires and may not support an organizational structure and methodology that has been established for the last two and a half centuries. Educational institutions may be broken up, a direction being seriously considered by many colleges and universities, that may overtake schools as well. In 2000-2001 56 percent of all two- and four-year degree granting colleges and universities offered distance education courses[3] At this writing, the largest colleges and universities in terms of enrollment may well be institutions that only operate as providers of distance education

For schools with boards and administrators brave enough (and prescient enough) to embrace the possibilities inherent in this view, there may be significant rewards. If all the students are not working in the same physical space and using faculty resources at the same time, a school can enroll more students, or use less space and fewer resources. Such a school could perhaps have a market advantage by lowering its cost! There will be a significant investment required to develop this highly distributed curriculum, along with evaluative tools to meet accreditation requirements and education for those involved with the process, but the payoff may be significant. The costs will be driven down if the school can sell its materials and processes on the open market (home schoolers are an obvious market), thus further increasing its competitive advantage.

Sooner or later the revolution promised by technology will overtake traditional education. It will take longer than it could take, but it will be shorter than most boards and educators believe. The empowerment of the individual to learn at her own pace and to satisfy her own creative intellectual curiosity without upsetting the syllabus is too powerful to delay for long. Boards responsible for the long-term health of their institutions need to pay attention to this transformative and ultimately disruptive process.

[1] *Merriam-Webster's Collegiate Dictionary, Eleventh Edition.* Springfield, MA: Merriam-Webster, Inc., 2003.
[2] *Ibid*
[3] nces.ed.gov/fastfacts

Appendix A

Essential School Elements: a loose Glossary

Most independent schools operate under section 501(c) (3) of the Internal Revenue Code and as such are not taxed on their income. Most states and cities follow that designation so that schools do not pay either income or sales tax. That is, of course, a subsidy which is in turn offset by: (a) parents' taxes that otherwise would support the education of their children which are available for other educational use; (b) service provided to communities in the form of space for community activities, volunteer efforts in the community by students and staff, and (c) the economic benefit to the community from the spending and taxes of faculty that live in the area and the value to local vendors, tradesmen and other suppliers to the institution.

The essential elements of a successful school are discussed below.

Administrative Staff

Apart from faculty and curriculum there are students to be recruited, funds to be raised, facilities to be maintained and cleaned, payrolls, bills to be paid, contracts to be negotiated and federal, state and local regulations and codes to be satisfied. Those functions, which may cost a fifth of the total school budget, are unavoidable if largely invisible.

One function of the administration of the school, which usually includes at least the head of school, business manager, division directors and directors of admissions and development, is to manage the various constituencies in support of the school's explicit mission. Of course, another function is the actual ongoing administration of the business of the school and management of faculty and administrative staff. It is worth noting here that heads of school, usually the only employees hired directly by the board of trustees, are almost always recruited from the academic ranks. Perhaps as compensation, in recent years, business managers have increasingly come from the for-profit world of business and not, as in earlier years, from the body of tired faculty members.

Board of Trustees

Part of the complication of an independent school is the variety of constituencies that have a stake in the success or failure of the institution. The board, in a legal sense, is the school, but in a practical sense it also serves as the lens for other external groups such as parents, alumni, friends and the community within which the school operates. The board ensures through its fiduciary oversight that the interests of these other constituencies are reflected in the mission and operation of the school and are preserved for the future. The primary responsibility of the board is to establish policies and provide oversight that will ensure the future health of the school.

Community

Schools exist within political jurisdictions, with neighbors and governments. Schools can and do ignore their private and public neighbors, but often at their peril. If they need to expand, change traffic patterns, or do any number of the normal things that schools do, they may need permits or permission; and if the communications and relationships are not already in place before there is a need, that need may be frustrated or delayed.

As in the other essential elements of a school, the political and neighborhood community must be paid attention to, and that takes interest, energy, planning and consistent implementation. It takes time, of course, away from other activities. Nevertheless, it is an essential task for the long term good of the school. Board members, often respected members of the community, bring a special capability with them to oversee and support good community relationships.

Clearly it is possible for elements necessary for successful operation of a school to be missing or in conflict. That represents a failure of the board to evaluate itself, its policies and the administrative officers hired to implement board policies. Most such failures result from a lack of clarity - clear, measurable goals - and rigorous evaluation of results in light of such goals. Leadership in such situations has failed.

Curriculum

The direct means by which educational content is "delivered" is determined by curriculum design. Curriculum design both determines and is limited by the budget, because the success of the design is largely determined by faculty quality and quantity. Curriculum also determines and is determined by facilities. A highly elective-based curriculum requires more classrooms and faculty than a highly structured core curriculum model. A media-oriented curriculum requires more expense for technology and training than a traditional, lecture-oriented curriculum. All choices have financial as well as curricular impact and the board ultimately will make those choices through its budget approval practices.

Facilities

Good facilities are those that effectively support program. While the "look" of an institution may not be a good measure of what goes on inside, it is hard to make a case that poor stewardship of facilities is unrelated to the quality of education within. As so many schools boast that they treat the whole child, so must an administration and board look to the whole institution as contributing to the education of its students.

Schools in recent years have poured large amounts of money into their facilities, as a result of heady economic times and the availability of cheap, tax-free, industrial revenue bonds. It is critical that ego-driven design issues not get in the way of the educative process. There must be sufficient teaching space so that curriculum is not shaped by facilities. There must be spaces for small groups, for music and art, for counseling, for athletics, for drama and for the myriad of other demands that are taken for granted in the best institutions (which attract the best teachers and students).

There must be consideration of the technology that is increasingly involved in education and, for that matter, in educational administration. There must be space for communication with prospective students, prospective donors and for parents and for administrators. It is difficult but important to trustees to inform themselves of the real and objective needs for space and to curb the universal tendency to overbuild and overspend for reasons not directly related to educational goals and needs.

Faculty

Education in American independent schools has traditionally been centrally controlled, not faculty controlled. In unionized public schools, that has been even more strongly the case, with extensive and expensive hierarchical administrative organizations.

Independent schools usually have been flat organizations and the head's control has been relatively absolute. That control is eroding for a number of reasons (discussed elsewhere), but it is, as a practical matter, impossible to control or even measure what goes on between a teacher and a student. In a very real sense, our schools are what happens at the furthest reaches of the interaction of those two individuals in class, on the playing field, in the cafeteria or elsewhere.

Faculty are also difficult to control directly because of their fragility. Paradoxically, faculty cherish independence while demanding dependence in the form of long-term relationships, extra benefits relating to tenure and family size, etc. It is important to understand that administrations and boards may control faculty by manipulating their physical dependence at the same time as they tout their intellectual independence.

Faculty, on the other hand, have a long tradition of manipulating schools. They understand that the school survives on their willingness to do a variety of jobs in and out of the classroom and that evaluation criteria are vague, if they exist at all. Wrongful termination suits are the major source of litigation in schools and they are very expensive to defend. Schools tend to try to keep faculty happy; when it is felt necessary to remove a faculty member, it is far more often by "counseling out" than by termination. Faculty members understand that and some use that fear for their own advantage.

School faculties tend to be well educated, of course, Democratic in their politics and largely female. Traditional democratic issues such as justice and equity, which are also often feminist issues, are always below or at the surface when compensation and benefits are on the table. Discussions are complicated and sometimes divisive since some of the issues pit faculty against one another. Should a school subsidize health insurance for families at the same level as for individuals or at the same percentage? What about health insurance for partners of employees? Is it fair to teachers without children if children of married couples are given a free education at the school?

The faculty is the school in a real sense, but the faculty presents the same kind of complicated problems that other areas of the school do and takes an enormous amount of energy and time and thought to manage and support successfully. While the direct responsibility for faculty belongs to the administration, faculty commitment and success is also affected by clarity of mission and the financial resources provided by the board to support that mission.

Finance

Once a school is established at a given enrollment, staff is hired and ancillary support services are designed. Budgets are constructed to support staff and services. Budgets are also the means by which funds are allocated among competing needs and by which the orderly expenditures for goods and services are controlled. Financial information, even in the small businesses that are schools, is fairly complicated. The chart of accounts is likely to be extensive; and the balance sheet accounts, alone, will be daunting due to the complications of accounting for "permanently" (donor) restricted funds, "temporarily restricted" funds, "unrestricted" funds and the treatment of gifts, all of which are artifacts of the Financial Accounting Standards Board and look nothing like the financial model most board members are used to. The ability to accumulate permanent restricted funds (endowment) through donations is a significant benefit of a charitable organization. Raising those funds and managing them well to support and ensure the future of the organization is a major responsibility of the board of trustees.

Friends

Not all board members come from the ranks of parents or former students. People from the community may become involved for a variety of reasons. Outside board members can play roles that a board or administration may desire. As "outsiders" they bring a different view from insiders, perhaps more objective than others and therefore valuable.

Graduates

A constituency that is generally more important to boarding schools than for day schools, they nonetheless have potential for fundraising that may be significant. Parents will transfer their philanthropic largess to the next school or college; graduates may well treasure their experience for their entire lifetime. They, too, may have loyalties to their colleges and universities, but many will hold their prep school in a special place and be meaningful donors. They are an important constituency because of the immediateness of their relationship to the school, although it may be hard to let them go as students and accept them as interested adults. Their relationship to the school is close and needs to be kept so, but they are hard to stay involved with and, of course, their relationship changes as their lives change, so management must change as well.

Parents

Parents are not only the people who choose the school (or support the choice of their children) and pay the bills, but who once in the school community want to have a role in its management. In the bad old days, long-term founder-heads might say, "This is my school; if you don't like it, take your child elsewhere." School heads mostly do not say that any more. They are more likely to work with parents and invite them into some kind of partnership, either because they see that as part of how the school works (see the chapter on Mission) or because they need to raise money from the parents above tuition to support the school's program.

In the last decade parents have become educated consumers of education services. They know far more about their school than most boards and administrators believe (and wish). They are partners, invited or not. As such, they are a constituency that requires attention and thought. Their role, like the role of the board, needs goals and evaluation, to which most schools pay little attention.